Nourish and Heal: Easy Homemade Meals For Cats and Dogs With Digestive Issues

James C. Tanner

Published by Calico GOLD, 2024.

While every precaution has been taken in the preparation of this book, the publisher assumes no responsibility for errors or omissions, or for damages resulting from the use of the information contained herein.

NOURISH AND HEAL: EASY HOMEMADE MEALS FOR CATS AND DOGS WITH DIGESTIVE ISSUES

First edition. March 20, 2024.

Copyright © 2024 James C. Tanner.

ISBN: 979-8224138982

Written by James C. Tanner.

Dedication

This book is dedicated to Cleo. Cleo was one of the best dogs I have ever had the privilege of living with. She was a German Shorthaired Pointer mixed with a German Shepherd.

An amazing pet and great babysitter to my young children when they would nap on blankets on the living room floor. Cleo, without being trained to do this, would lay down beside my infant children and stay there, only leaving to come get us when the children began to wake up.

As wonderful as Cleo was, she did have her quirks. When near a pond, Cleo would dive in and immediately dive, trying to pull up rocks from the bottom of the pond. The problem was, she would always try to grab rocks that were too heavy for her to handle. She would stay under water for so long, I'd be stripped down to my underwear and about to dive in after her when she would surface dragging a massive rock with her.

Around the age of two years old, Cleo developed a digestive disorder. This disorder revealed her superpower – FARTS!

Cleo was the only dog I knew who, when in a crowded room, would quietly release gas, and within 2 to 3 minutes have people rushing out of the room thinking someone should call the fire department to have the HAZ MAT team attend so as to identify the source of such a noxious gas leak. Her farts did not smell like burning rubber. They stunk like the whole tire manufacturing plant was burning up. Every time Cleo farted, even she would get up and leave the room.

In the end, I had to put Cleo on a homemade diet, which worked amazingly well, along with biscuits that contained active charcoal to control the odour of the farts. Cleo lived 2 years longer than most German Shepherds or German Shorthair Pointers, and was very active and healthy right up until the end when a sudden kidney condition ended her life.

****

****

****

Introduction

Welcome to "Nourish to Heal: Easy Homemade Meals For Cats and Dogs With Digestive Issues," a guide dedicated to pet owners who are seeking to improve their furry companions' health through nutrition. As a past pet owner, I have witnessed firsthand the profound impact that diet can have on the well-being of our pets. Raised in a home that bred show quality dogs, and then moving on to attain post-secondary education in studies such as animal sciences, livestock production, and practical veterinary medicine, I can state emphatically that my whole life has been bathes in a love for animals and animal health. This book is the culmination of years of experience, research, and a deep-seated belief in the healing power of proper nutrition when fed to our pets.

Digestive disorders are among the most common health issues faced by cats and dogs. They can range from mild upsets to chronic conditions that significantly affect a pet's quality of life. Symptoms such as vomiting, diarrhea, constipation, and weight loss are not only distressing for our pets but also for us as their caregivers. Understanding the root causes of these symptoms and how to address them through diet is the first step towards nurturing a healthier, happier pet.

The journey to optimal digestive health begins with knowledge. In the chapters that follow, we will explore the various digestive disorders that can affect cats and dogs. By recognizing the signs and symptoms of these conditions, you can become a more informed and proactive advocate for your pet's health. We will delve into the medical conditions, diseases, and illnesses that are commonly associated with digestive issues in both species, providing a solid foundation for understanding the complexities of their digestive systems.

Nutrition is the cornerstone of good health, and this is especially true for pets with digestive disorders. A balanced diet is essential for supporting their overall well-being and aiding in the management of their conditions. We will discuss the nutritional requirements of cats and dogs, highlighting the importance of a diet that is tailored to their specific needs. Deciphering nutritional and ingredient labels on commercial pet food packaging is a crucial skill that we will develop, enabling you to make informed choices about what you feed your pet.

Unfortunately, commercial pet foods are not always as wholesome as they appear. We will unveil some of the hidden ingredients in these products and discuss the potential impact they can have on your pet's health. This knowledge will empower you to make the switch to homemade diets, which can be customized to address your pet's unique nutritional needs and preferences.

Creating a diet plan for a cat or dog with digestive issues requires careful consideration and planning. We will guide you through the process of crafting diets that not only meet their nutritional requirements but also support their digestive health. Meal planning and preparation tips will be provided to help you seamlessly integrate these dietary changes into your busy life.

Finally, we will share a collection of recipes for homemade cat and dog food, designed to be both nutritious and appealing to your pets. These recipes will serve as a starting point for you to experiment and create meals that your furry friends will love and thrive on.

"Nourish to Heal" is more than just a cookbook for pets; it is a comprehensive guide to understanding and addressing digestive issues through the power of nutrition. It is my hope that this book will inspire you to take an active role in your pet's health and well-being, leading to a happier and more vibrant life for both of you. Together, let's embark on this journey to nourish and heal our much loved pets.

****

Chapter 1

The Digestive Anatomy of Cats and Dogs

Welcome to the fascinating world of the digestive system in our beloved pets, cats and dogs. I have seen firsthand the crucial role that the digestive system plays in the overall health and well-being of our furry companions. As we begin the detailed learning processes contained in this book, we will begin our journey by understanding the basic anatomy and physiology of the digestive system in both species, highlighting the key organs and their functions.

The Mouth and Teeth: The Beginning of Digestion

Welcome to the first step in the digestive journey of our beloved cats and dogs. As a one time pet-owner of pets with serious digestive disorders, I've come to appreciate the significance of every part of the digestive system, starting with the mouth and teeth. Let's begin our understanding by exploring where digestion begins... in the mouth, where food is taken in and mechanically broken down by the teeth, and how the saliva produced in the mouth plays a crucial role in the digestive process.

The mouth, or oral cavity, is the entry point for food and the first site of digestion. It's equipped with various structures that aid in the breakdown of food, preparing it for further digestion in the stomach and intestines. The lips, tongue, and teeth all work together to grasp, chew, and mix the food with saliva, initiating the digestive process.

Cats and dogs are carnivores by nature, and their teeth are designed to reflect their dietary needs. They have sharp, pointed canines for tearing meat and strong molars for grinding and crushing food. Each type of tooth has a specific function:

1. **Incisors**: These are the small front teeth used for nibbling and grooming.
2. **Canines**: The long, pointed teeth used for tearing and gripping food.
3. **Premolars and Molars**: The larger teeth at the back of the mouth used for grinding and crushing food.

The arrangement and shape of teeth in cats and dogs are adapted for their carnivorous diets, allowing them to efficiently break down meat and other tough materials. However, domestication has led to changes in their diets, and many pets now consume commercial pet foods that may not require the same level of mechanical breakdown.

Saliva is more than just moisture; it's a complex fluid containing water, electrolytes, mucus, and enzymes. The primary enzyme in saliva is amylase, which begins the chemical breakdown of carbohydrates into simpler sugars. While dogs produce a significant amount of amylase in their saliva, cats produce very little, reflecting their natural high-protein, low-carbohydrate diet.

Saliva also serves several other important functions in the mouth:

- **Lubrication**: It helps moisten food, making it easier to swallow and reducing the risk of choking.
- **Protection**: Saliva helps neutralize acids and provides a barrier against bacteria and viruses, protecting the teeth and gums from infection.
- **Taste**: It dissolves food particles, allowing them to interact with taste receptors on the tongue.

The tongue is a muscular organ that plays a crucial role in the feeding process. It helps position food between the teeth for chewing and forms the chewed food into a bolus (a small, round mass) for swallowing. The tongue also contains taste buds, which are essential for detecting the flavors of food, and can influence appetite and food preferences.

In cats, the tongue has a unique feature called papillae, which are tiny, backward-facing barbs. These papillae give the tongue a rough texture and are useful for grooming fur and scraping meat off bones.

Chewing, or mastication, is the process of breaking down food into smaller pieces using the teeth and jaw muscles. This mechanical digestion increases the surface area of the food, making it more accessible to digestive enzymes later in the process. Chewing also mixes the food with saliva, which starts the chemical breakdown of carbohydrates and makes the food easier to swallow.

Once the food is adequately chewed and mixed with saliva, it's ready to be swallowed. Swallowing, or deglutition, is a complex process that involves the coordinated action of the tongue, soft palate, and throat muscles. The epiglottis, a small flap of tissue, closes over the trachea (windpipe) to prevent food from entering the airways. The bolus of food is then pushed into the esophagus, the muscular tube that connects the mouth to the stomach, marking the end of the oral phase of digestion.

The mouth and teeth play a crucial role in the digestive process, providing the first step in breaking down food into a form that can be further digested and absorbed by the body. Understanding the anatomy and functions of the mouth, teeth, and saliva is essential for recognizing when something goes wrong and how to address it. As we move through the digestive system in the following chapters, we'll see how each part contributes to the overall health and well-being of our pets.

The Esophagus: The Food Conduit

Welcome to the next stop in our exploration of the digestive system of cats and dogs: the esophagus. After food is sufficiently chewed and mixed with saliva in the mouth, it is swallowed and begins its journey down this critical yet often overlooked structure. In this section, we will delve into the anatomy and function of the esophagus, the role of peristaltic movements in transporting food, and some common esophageal disorders that can affect our furry companions.

The esophagus is a muscular tube that connects the throat (pharynx) to the stomach. In dogs and cats, it is approximately 25 to 40 centimeters long, depending on the size of the animal. The esophagus is composed of several layers:

1. **Mucosa**: The innermost layer, lined with a smooth, protective epithelium that helps food slide easily.
2. **Submucosa**: A connective tissue layer that contains blood vessels, nerves, and glands that produce mucus.
3. **Muscularis**: The muscular layer responsible for the peristaltic movements that propel food. It consists of both circular and longitudinal muscle fibers.
4. **Adventitia**: The outermost layer that connects the esophagus to surrounding tissues.

The esophagus passes through the neck, chest cavity, and diaphragm before entering the stomach. At the junction where the esophagus meets the stomach, there is a ring-like muscle called the lower esophageal sphincter (LES). The LES acts as a valve, opening to allow food to enter the stomach and closing to prevent stomach contents from flowing back into the esophagus.

Swallowing is a complex process that involves the coordination of muscles in the mouth, pharynx, and esophagus. Once food is swallowed, it enters the esophagus, where the real journey begins. The process of moving food through the esophagus to the stomach is called peristalsis. This involves a series of coordinated, wave-like contractions of the esophageal muscles.

Peristalsis starts as a reflex action triggered by the act of swallowing. The muscles contract behind the food bolus, creating pressure that pushes it forward, while the muscles ahead of the bolus relax, allowing the esophagus to expand and accommodate the moving food. These contractions are smooth and continuous, propelling the food from the throat to the stomach in a matter of seconds.

While peristalsis is the primary force that moves food through the esophagus, gravity also plays a role, especially in animals like dogs and cats that often eat with their heads lowered. The vertical orientation of the esophagus in this position aids in the downward movement of food. However, even when an animal is lying down or in an unusual position, peristalsis can still effectively transport food to the stomach.

The esophagus plays a vital role in the digestive process, serving as the conduit that transports food from the mouth to the stomach. Understanding the anatomy and function of the esophagus, as well as the potential disorders that can affect it, is essential for maintaining the digestive health of cats and dogs. As we continue our journey through the digestive system, we will see how each component works together to nourish and sustain our beloved pets.

The Stomach: A Chemical Processing Chamber

Welcome to the next stage in the digestive journey of our feline and canine companions: the stomach. This muscular organ is not just a simple holding tank for food; it is a complex chemical processing chamber where the initial stages of protein digestion occur. In this section, we will explore the anatomy and function of the stomach, the role of gastric juices in digestion, and how the stomach adapts to the dietary habits of dogs and cats.

The stomach is located between the esophagus and the small intestine. It has a curved shape and is divided into several regions:

1. **Cardia**: The area where the esophagus meets the stomach. It contains the lower esophageal sphincter, which prevents the backflow of stomach contents.
2. **Fundus**: The upper dome-shaped part of the stomach that stores undigested food and gases.
3. **Body**: The largest section of the stomach, where gastric juices mix with food to begin digestion.
4. **Pylorus**: The lower part of the stomach that connects to the small intestine. It contains the pyloric sphincter, which regulates the passage of partially digested food into the small intestine.

The stomach wall is composed of several layers, including the mucosa (inner lining), submucosa, muscularis (muscle layer), and serosa (outer layer). The mucosa contains glands that produce gastric juices, while the muscularis is responsible for the churning and mixing actions of the stomach.

Gastric juices are a mixture of hydrochloric acid, digestive enzymes, and mucus. They play a crucial role in the digestive process:

1. **Hydrochloric Acid (HCl)**: This acid creates an acidic environment in the stomach, which is necessary for the activation of digestive enzymes. It also helps kill bacteria and other pathogens in the food.

2. **Pepsin**: This enzyme is responsible for breaking down proteins into smaller peptides. It is activated by the acidic environment created by HCl.
3. **Lipase**: Although present in small amounts, this enzyme helps break down fats.
4. **Mucus**: Produced by specialized cells in the stomach lining, mucus protects the stomach wall from the corrosive effects of the acid and enzymes.

The production and secretion of gastric juices are regulated by neural and hormonal signals. When food enters the stomach, the presence of proteins and the stretching of the stomach wall trigger the release of gastrin, a hormone that stimulates the production of gastric juices.

Once food enters the stomach, it is mixed with gastric juices to form a semi-liquid mixture called chyme. The stomach's muscular walls contract in a rhythmic manner, churning and mixing the chyme to ensure thorough digestion. This process is known as gastric motility.

The acidic environment in the stomach also serves to denature proteins, making them more accessible for enzymatic breakdown. Additionally, the acidity helps to break down connective tissues in meat, softening it and making it easier to digest.

There are some notable differences in the size and function of the stomach between dogs and cats:

1. **Dogs**: Canines have a more expandable stomach that can accommodate large meals. This is an evolutionary adaptation to their ancestral feeding habits, which involved consuming large quantities of food when available and fasting when food was scarce. The stomach of a dog can expand significantly after a meal, allowing them to ingest and store a considerable amount of food for gradual digestion.

2. **Cats**: Felines, on the other hand, have a smaller stomach suited to their natural feeding pattern of frequent, smaller meals throughout the day. This reflects their evolutionary background as solitary hunters who would catch and consume smaller prey.

The stomach plays a pivotal role in the digestive process, serving as a chemical processing chamber where the breakdown of proteins begins. Understanding the anatomy and function of the stomach, as well as the common disorders that can affect it, is crucial for maintaining the digestive health.

The Small Intestine: The Hub of Nutrient Absorption

After the initial stages of digestion in the stomach, the semi-liquid mixture called chyme moves into the small intestine, the central stage of the digestive process. This vital organ is not only the longest part of the digestive tract but also the primary site for nutrient absorption. In this section, we will explore the structure and function of the small intestine, the role of villi in nutrient absorption, and the contributions of the pancreas and liver to the digestive process.

The small intestine is a long, coiled tube that extends from the stomach to the large intestine. It is divided into three sections:

1. **Duodenum**: The first and shortest section, which receives chyme from the stomach, along with digestive enzymes and bile.
2. **Jejunum**: The middle section, where the majority of nutrient absorption occurs.
3. **Ileum**: The final section, which continues the process of absorption and connects to the large intestine.

In dogs and cats, the small intestine can be several meters long, with the length varying depending on the size of the animal. Despite its length, the small intestine is compactly arranged within the abdominal cavity.

The inner lining of the small intestine is covered with tiny, finger-like projections called villi. These structures greatly increase the surface area for absorption, allowing for more efficient nutrient uptake. Each villus contains a network of capillaries and a lymphatic vessel, which transport absorbed nutrients into the bloodstream and lymphatic system, respectively.

In addition to villi, the surface of the small intestine also features microvilli, even smaller projections on the surface of intestinal cells. Together, villi and microvilli form the brush border, which further enhances the absorptive capacity of the small intestine.

The pancreas and liver play crucial roles in the digestive process by secreting enzymes and bile into the small intestine:

1. **Pancreatic Enzymes**: The pancreas produces a variety of enzymes that are essential for breaking down different types of nutrients:
   - **Proteases** (such as trypsin and chymotrypsin) break down proteins into amino acids.
   - **Amylase** breaks down carbohydrates into simple sugars.
   - **Lipases** break down fats into fatty acids and glycerol.
2. **Bile**: Produced by the liver and stored in the gallbladder, bile is released into the small intestine to help emulsify fats. Emulsification is the process of breaking down large fat droplets into smaller ones, increasing their surface area for lipase action. Bile also aids in the absorption of fat-soluble vitamins (A, D, E, and K).

The combined action of pancreatic enzymes and bile ensures the efficient breakdown and absorption of nutrients in the small intestine.

As the chyme moves through the small intestine, nutrients are absorbed through the walls of the intestine and into the bloodstream. The absorption process varies depending on the type of nutrient:

1. **Carbohydrates**: Broken down into simple sugars, such as glucose, which are absorbed by the cells lining the small intestine and transported into the bloodstream.
2. **Proteins**: Broken down into amino acids, which are absorbed and used by the body for various functions, including tissue repair and enzyme production.
3. **Fats**: Emulsified by bile and broken down by lipases into fatty acids and glycerol, which are absorbed into the lymphatic system before entering the bloodstream.
4. **Vitamins and Minerals**: Absorbed in different parts of the small intestine, with fat-soluble vitamins absorbed along with fats and water-soluble vitamins absorbed directly into the bloodstream.

The small intestine is a marvel of the digestive system, playing a central role in the breakdown and absorption of nutrients. Understanding the structure and function of the small intestine, along with the contributions of the pancreas and liver, is essential for maintaining the digestive health of cats and dogs.

The Large Intestine: Water Absorption and Waste Formation

After the meticulous process of digestion and nutrient absorption in the small intestine, the remaining undigested material moves into the large intestine, also known as the colon. This final segment of the digestive tract plays a crucial role in water absorption, electrolyte balance, and the formation of feces. In this chapter, we will explore the anatomy and function of the large intestine, the importance of gut bacteria, and how this organ contributes to the overall health of cats and dogs.

Anatomy of the Large Intestine

The large intestine is shorter in length than the small intestine but has a larger diameter. It is divided into several parts:

1. **Cecum**: A small pouch at the junction of the small and large intestines, where fermentation of undigested material begins.
2. **Colon**: The main section of the large intestine, divided into ascending, transverse, descending, and sigmoid segments in humans. In dogs and cats, the colon is less distinctly segmented but still serves the same functions.
3. **Rectum**: The final section of the large intestine, where feces are stored before being expelled through the anus.

The large intestine has a lining similar to that of the small intestine, but with fewer villi, as its primary function is not absorption of nutrients but rather water and electrolytes.

One of the primary functions of the large intestine is to absorb water and electrolytes from the undigested material, transforming it from a liquid or semi-liquid state into a more solid form known as feces. This process is essential for maintaining the body's fluid and electrolyte balance.

As the material moves through the colon, water is absorbed through the intestinal walls and into the bloodstream. This process gradually thickens the material, forming it into feces. The rate of transit through the large intestine can affect the consistency of the feces; slower transit times result in more water absorption and harder stools, while faster transit times lead to less absorption and softer stools.

The Role of Gut Bacteria

The large intestine, or colon, is more than just the final stretch of the digestive tract; it is a bustling ecosystem teeming with trillions of bacteria. This community of microorganisms, known collectively as the gut microbiota, plays a crucial role in the health and well-being of cats and dogs. Here, we'll explore the fascinating world of gut bacteria, examining their functions in fermentation, vitamin synthesis, and immune system support.

While the small intestine is the primary site for nutrient absorption, some undigested carbohydrates and dietary fibers make their way to the large intestine. Here, they undergo fermentation by gut bacteria. This process involves the breakdown of these substances into simpler compounds, primarily short-chain fatty acids (SCFAs) such as acetate, propionate, and butyrate.

Short-chain fatty acids serve several important functions:

1. **Energy Source for Colon Cells**: SCFAs, particularly butyrate, are a vital energy source for the cells lining the colon. They help maintain the health and integrity of the intestinal barrier, which is crucial for preventing the entry of harmful substances into the bloodstream.
2. **Regulation of Inflammation**: SCFAs have anti-inflammatory properties and play a role in regulating the immune response within the gut.
3. **Appetite Regulation**: Some SCFAs can influence the release of appetite-regulating hormones, potentially impacting the feeding behavior and weight of the animal.

Gut bacteria are capable of synthesizing certain vitamins that are essential for the health of cats and dogs. These include:

1. **Vitamin K**: Important for blood clotting and bone health. While cats and dogs can obtain vitamin K from their diet, the synthesis of this vitamin by gut bacteria provides an additional source.

2. **B Vitamins**: Some members of the gut microbiota can produce B vitamins, including folate (B9), biotin (B7), and cobalamin (B12). These vitamins play crucial roles in energy metabolism, nerve function, and red blood cell production.

The vitamins produced by gut bacteria are absorbed into the bloodstream, contributing to the overall nutritional status of the animal.

One of the most vital roles of the gut microbiota is its contribution to the immune system. The large intestine is a key site of immune activity, and the bacteria that reside there are in constant communication with the body's immune cells. This interaction helps to:

1. **Protect Against Pathogens**: Beneficial bacteria in the gut can outcompete harmful pathogens for nutrients and space, effectively preventing them from establishing a foothold. They also produce substances that can inhibit or kill harmful bacteria.

2. **Regulate Inflammation**: The gut microbiota helps to regulate the body's inflammatory response. Certain bacteria can produce short-chain fatty acids (SCFAs) like butyrate, which have anti-inflammatory properties and can help to modulate the immune response.

3. **Develop Immune Tolerance**: Exposure to a diverse range of bacteria in the gut helps the immune system to distinguish between harmful and harmless substances. This is particularly important in preventing overreactions to non-harmful antigens, which can lead to allergies and autoimmune

diseases.

The Rectum and Anus: The End of the Digestive Journey

The final stage of digestion occurs in the rectum, where feces are stored until they are expelled through the anus. The process of defecation is controlled by voluntary and involuntary muscles, allowing the animal to eliminate waste at an appropriate time and place.

Cats have some unique features in their digestive system. They are obligate carnivores, meaning their diet must consist primarily of meat. Their digestive tract is shorter and more acidic than that of dogs, reflecting their adaptation to a high-protein, low-carbohydrate diet. Cats also have a limited ability to digest certain carbohydrates, which is why a diet high in animal proteins is essential for their health.

Dogs, on the other hand, are more omnivorous and can digest a wider variety of foods, including some grains and vegetables. Their digestive system is more adaptable, allowing them to thrive on a more varied diet. However, this does not mean that all foods are suitable for dogs; their diet still needs to be carefully balanced to meet their nutritional needs.

Understanding the basic anatomy and physiology of the digestive system in cats and dogs is the foundation for recognizing when something goes wrong and how to address it. A healthy digestive system is crucial for the overall well-being of your pet, as it is responsible for breaking down food, absorbing nutrients, and eliminating waste. In the following chapters, we will delve deeper into common digestive disorders, the importance of balanced nutrition, and how to craft diets that support digestive health in our feline and canine friends.

****

Chapter 2

Understanding Digestive Disorders in Cats and Dogs:

A General Introduction To The Topic

The digestive system is a vital network that performs the crucial task of converting food into energy and nutrients. These nutrients are then absorbed and used to support every function in the body, from growth and repair to immune defense. A healthy digestive system is essential for maintaining the overall health and vitality of our pets.

Let's tip-toe our way into this subject matter by looking at, in a very general sense, some of the disorders that impact both cats and dogs. This is by no means a complete list.

Common Digestive Disorders

Digestive disorders can range from mild, transient upsets to severe, chronic conditions that require lifelong management. Some of the most common issues include:

- **Acute Gastroenteritis**: Inflammation of the stomach and intestines, often resulting in vomiting and diarrhea. This can be caused by dietary indiscretion, infections, or toxins.
- **Inflammatory Bowel Disease (IBD)**: A chronic condition characterized by persistent inflammation of the gastrointestinal tract, leading to symptoms like weight loss, vomiting, and diarrhea.
- **Pancreatitis**: Inflammation of the pancreas, which can be acute or chronic, and can severely impact digestion and nutrient absorption.
- **Liver Disease**: The liver plays a crucial role in digestion and

metabolism. Disorders affecting the liver can have significant repercussions on digestive health.

Symptoms to Watch Out For

Early detection is key in managing digestive disorders. Pet owners should be vigilant for signs such as:

- **Vomiting**: While occasional vomiting may not be a cause for alarm, frequent or persistent vomiting requires veterinary attention.
- **Diarrhea**: Persistent diarrhea can lead to dehydration and nutrient loss, warranting a thorough investigation.
- **Weight Loss**: Unexplained weight loss, especially if accompanied by other digestive symptoms, can be a sign of a chronic digestive disorder.
- **Changes in Appetite**: A sudden increase or decrease in appetite can indicate digestive issues.
- **Abdominal Pain or Distension**: Swelling or tenderness in the belly area can be a sign of serious digestive problems.

Diagnosing Digestive Disorders

Diagnosing digestive disorders involves a combination of clinical examination, medical history, and diagnostic tests such as:

- **Blood Tests**: To assess organ function and detect inflammation or infection.
- **Fecal Examinations**: To check for parasites and other pathogens.
- **Imaging**: X-rays or ultrasound can help visualize internal structures and identify abnormalities.
- **Endoscopy**: A more invasive procedure that allows direct

visualization of the gastrointestinal tract.

Understanding Digestive Disorders, Chronic Diseases, and Illnesses in Cats and Dogs

One of the most common questions I encounter is about the distinction between a digestive disorder, a chronic digestive disease, and a digestive illness in pets. While these terms are often used interchangeably, they do have distinct meanings that are important to understand for effective diagnosis and management.

A digestive disorder is a broad term that encompasses any condition that negatively affects the functioning of the digestive system. This can include acute issues like dietary indiscretions leading to vomiting or diarrhea, as well as more chronic conditions such as inflammatory bowel disease (IBD). Essentially, a disorder refers to any abnormality or disturbance in the normal digestive process.

Chronic digestive diseases are a subset of digestive disorders that persist over an extended period, often for the life of the pet. These conditions are usually characterized by ongoing symptoms that may fluctuate in severity but never fully resolve. Examples include:

- **Inflammatory Bowel Disease (IBD)**: A group of disorders characterized by chronic inflammation of the gastrointestinal tract.
- **Chronic Pancreatitis**: Long-term inflammation of the pancreas that disrupts its normal functioning.
- **Liver Disease**: Conditions such as hepatitis or cirrhosis that affect the liver's ability to perform its vital roles in digestion and metabolism.

Chronic diseases often require ongoing management, including dietary modifications, medications, and regular monitoring by a veterinarian.

Digestive illnesses typically refer to acute or short-term conditions that affect the digestive system. These can be caused by infections, dietary indiscretions, or exposure to toxins. Examples include:

- **Gastroenteritis**: Inflammation of the stomach and intestines, often resulting in vomiting and diarrhea. This can be caused by viral or bacterial infections, parasites, or ingestion of spoiled food or foreign objects.
- **Parasitic Infections**: Conditions like giardiasis or roundworm infestation that disrupt normal digestion and nutrient absorption.
- **Food Poisoning**: Illness resulting from ingesting toxins or contaminated food.

Digestive illnesses often require immediate but temporary treatment, and the prognosis is usually good with prompt veterinary care.

Key Differences Between Disorders, Diseases, and Illnesses:

1. **Duration**: Disorders can be acute or chronic, diseases are typically chronic, and illnesses are usually acute.
2. **Management**: Chronic diseases often require lifelong management, while illnesses generally require short-term treatment.
3. **Prognosis**: The prognosis for acute illnesses is usually favorable with treatment, while chronic diseases may have a more guarded prognosis due to their ongoing nature.

Regardless of the classification, it's crucial to recognize the signs of digestive issues in your pet. Symptoms like vomiting, diarrhea, loss of appetite, or abdominal pain should prompt a visit to the veterinarian. Early diagnosis and treatment are key to managing digestive disorders, diseases, and illnesses effectively.

Understanding the distinctions between digestive disorders, chronic diseases, and illnesses is essential for providing the best care for our pets. By recognizing the differences in duration, management, and prognosis, pet owners and veterinarians can work together to ensure that cats and dogs with digestive issues receive the appropriate treatment and support they need to lead healthy, happy lives.

****

Chapter 3

Digestive Medical Conditions, Diseases, and Illnesses Common to Cats

Mouth Related

These conditions can significantly impact a cat's ability to eat and, consequently, their overall health. In this section, we'll delve into some of the most common oral health problems in felines, exploring their causes, diagnosis, treatment, and prognosis.

1. Periodontal Disease

Etiology: Periodontal disease is the most common dental condition in cats. It begins with the formation of plaque on the teeth, which hardens into tartar. Bacteria in the tartar can infect the gums and the structures supporting the teeth, leading to inflammation, tooth loss, and systemic health issues.

Diagnosis: A thorough oral examination, often under anesthesia, is required to diagnose periodontal disease. Dental radiographs may be necessary to assess the extent of the disease.

Treatment: Treatment involves professional dental cleaning to remove plaque and tartar, followed by regular home dental care. In advanced cases, extraction of affected teeth may be necessary.

Prognosis: With early detection and proper treatment, the prognosis for cats with periodontal disease is generally good. However, ongoing dental care is essential to prevent recurrence.

2. Stomatitis

Etiology: Feline stomatitis is a severe, painful inflammation of the mouth and gums. Its exact cause is unknown, but it is believed to be an immune-mediated response to plaque or other oral antigens.

Diagnosis: Diagnosis is based on clinical signs and oral examination. Biopsies may be performed to rule out other conditions.

Treatment: Treatment often involves extensive dental extractions to remove sources of inflammation. Anti-inflammatory medications and pain management are also important. In some cases, immunosuppressive drugs may be used.

Prognosis: Stomatitis can be challenging to manage, and long-term treatment may be necessary. The prognosis varies, with some cats responding well to treatment and others requiring ongoing care.

3. Tooth Resorption

Etiology: Tooth resorption is a common condition in cats, characterized by the progressive destruction of tooth structure. The exact cause is unknown, but it is believed to be related to factors such as age, diet, and oral health.

Diagnosis: It is often diagnosed during routine dental examinations. Dental radiographs are essential for assessing the extent of the resorption.

Treatment: Treatment typically involves the extraction of affected teeth. Pain management is also crucial.

Prognosis: With appropriate treatment, the prognosis for cats with tooth resorption is generally good. However, regular dental check-ups are necessary to monitor for new lesions.

4. Oral Tumors

Etiology: Oral tumors in cats can be benign or malignant, with squamous cell carcinoma being the most common malignant tumor. Risk factors may include exposure to tobacco smoke, certain viruses, and genetic predisposition.

Diagnosis: Diagnosis involves a thorough oral examination and biopsy of the tumor. Imaging studies may be needed to assess the extent of the disease.

Treatment: Treatment depends on the type and location of the tumor. Surgery, radiation therapy, and chemotherapy may be options.

Prognosis: The prognosis for cats with oral tumors varies widely depending on the type and stage of the tumor. Early detection and treatment are crucial for a better outcome.

5. Gingivitis

Etiology: Gingivitis is the inflammation of the gums, often caused by the accumulation of plaque and tartar. It can also be associated with systemic diseases such as feline immunodeficiency virus (FIV) and feline leukemia virus (FeLV).

Diagnosis: A visual examination of the gums can reveal redness, swelling, and bleeding, indicating gingivitis. Further tests may be required to diagnose underlying systemic conditions.

Treatment: Treatment involves professional dental cleaning to remove plaque and tartar, followed by regular home dental care. Addressing any underlying systemic conditions is also important.

Prognosis: With proper treatment and ongoing dental care, the prognosis for cats with gingivitis is generally good. However, without proper care, it can progress to more severe periodontal disease.

Mouth-related digestive issues in cats are not only common but can also have a significant impact on their quality of life. Early detection and appropriate treatment are key to managing these conditions and ensuring the overall well-being of our feline friends. Regular veterinary check-ups, including dental examinations, are essential for maintaining optimal oral health in cats. As cat owners, it's crucial to be vigilant about your pet's oral hygiene and seek veterinary care at the first sign of any dental problems.

The Esophagus

The esophagus is a crucial component of the digestive system, responsible for transporting food from the mouth to the stomach. In cats, several conditions can affect the esophagus, leading to discomfort, difficulty swallowing, and other symptoms. In this section, we will explore the most common esophagus-related digestive issues in cats, including their causes, diagnosis, treatment, and prognosis.

1. Esophagitis

Etiology: Esophagitis is the inflammation of the esophagus, often caused by acid reflux, foreign body ingestion, or anesthesia-related complications. It can also result from infections or certain medications.

Diagnosis: Diagnosis typically involves endoscopy, which allows direct visualization of the esophageal lining. Biopsies may be taken to assess the extent of inflammation and rule out other conditions.

Treatment: Treatment focuses on addressing the underlying cause, managing symptoms, and protecting the esophageal lining. This may include antacids, gastroprotectants, and anti-inflammatory medications. Dietary management, such as feeding a bland, easily digestible diet, can also be beneficial.

Prognosis: The prognosis for cats with esophagitis is generally good if the underlying cause is identified and appropriately managed. However, chronic or severe cases may lead to complications such as strictures.

2. Esophageal Obstruction

Etiology: Esophageal obstruction, or foreign body impaction, occurs when an object becomes lodged in the esophagus. Common culprits include bones, toys, or hairballs. Cats with esophageal strictures or motility disorders are at higher risk for obstructions.

Diagnosis: Clinical signs such as regurgitation, drooling, and distress are suggestive of an obstruction. Imaging studies, such as X-rays or endoscopy, are used to confirm the diagnosis and locate the obstruction.

Treatment: Treatment involves the removal of the foreign object, which may be achieved through endoscopy or, in some cases, surgery. Supportive care, including hydration and pain management, is also important.

Prognosis: With prompt treatment, the prognosis for cats with esophageal obstructions is generally good. However, delays in treatment or complications can lead to more serious outcomes.

3. Esophageal Strictures

Etiology: Esophageal strictures are the narrowing of the esophagus, often resulting from chronic inflammation, injury, or acid reflux. They can lead to difficulty swallowing and regurgitation.

Diagnosis: Strictures can be diagnosed using endoscopy or contrast radiography, which allows visualization of the narrowed area.

Treatment: Treatment often involves esophageal dilation, a procedure to stretch the narrowed area. This may need to be repeated multiple times. Medications to reduce acid reflux and inflammation may also be prescribed.

Prognosis: The prognosis for cats with esophageal strictures varies depending on the severity and response to treatment. In some cases, strictures can recur, requiring ongoing management.

4. Megaesophagus

Etiology: Megaesophagus is characterized by the dilation and decreased motility of the esophagus. It can be congenital or acquired, with potential causes including neuromuscular disorders, infections, or idiopathic (unknown) factors.

Diagnosis: Clinical signs such as regurgitation and weight loss, along with radiographic evidence of an enlarged esophagus, support the diagnosis of megaesophagus.

Treatment: Treatment focuses on managing symptoms and addressing any underlying causes. Feeding modifications, such as offering small, frequent meals from an elevated position, can help reduce regurgitation.

Prognosis: The prognosis for cats with megaesophagus varies depending on the underlying cause and the severity of the condition. In some cases, it can be managed effectively with dietary and lifestyle changes.

5. Gastroesophageal Reflux Disease (GERD)

Etiology: GERD occurs when stomach acid flows back into the esophagus, causing irritation and inflammation. It can be triggered by factors such as anesthesia, obesity, or hiatal hernias.

Diagnosis: Diagnosis is often based on clinical signs and response to treatment. Endoscopy may be used to assess the extent of esophageal damage.

Treatment: Treatment includes dietary management, such as feeding smaller, more frequent meals, and medications to reduce stomach acid and protect the esophageal lining.

Prognosis: With appropriate treatment, the prognosis for cats with GERD is generally good. However, long-term management may be necessary to prevent recurrence.

Esophagus-related digestive issues in cats can range from mild to severe, impacting their ability to eat and maintain proper nutrition. Early recognition and prompt veterinary care are essential for effective treatment and a positive outcome. Regular check-ups and attention to changes in eating behavior can help catch these conditions early, ensuring a swift and successful recovery. As always, maintaining open communication with your veterinarian is key to keeping your feline friend healthy and happy.

The Stomach

The stomach is a critical component of the digestive system, responsible for the initial breakdown of food. In cats, various conditions can affect the stomach, leading to a range of symptoms and potential complications.

1. Gastritis

Etiology: Gastritis refers to the inflammation of the stomach lining. It can be acute or chronic and is often caused by dietary indiscretion, infections, toxins, or stress. Chronic gastritis may also be associated with underlying health conditions, such as kidney disease or inflammatory bowel disease (IBD).

Diagnosis: Diagnosis involves a combination of clinical signs, blood tests, and imaging studies. Endoscopy is the gold standard for assessing the extent of inflammation and obtaining tissue samples for biopsy.

Treatment: Treatment focuses on addressing the underlying cause and providing supportive care. This may include dietary changes, antiemetics, antacids, and gastroprotectants. In cases of chronic gastritis, long-term management may be necessary.

Prognosis: The prognosis for cats with gastritis varies depending on the cause and severity. Acute gastritis often resolves with appropriate treatment, while chronic gastritis may require ongoing management.

2. Gastric Ulcers

Etiology: Gastric ulcers are lesions that form in the stomach lining. They can be caused by prolonged use of nonsteroidal anti-inflammatory drugs (NSAIDs), stress, infections, or underlying diseases that increase stomach acidity.

Diagnosis: Ulcers are diagnosed through endoscopy, which allows for direct visualization of the lesions. Blood tests and imaging studies may also be used to assess the cat's overall health and identify any contributing factors.

Treatment: Treatment aims to reduce stomach acid and protect the ulcerated area. This may include proton pump inhibitors, H2 receptor antagonists, and sucralfate. Addressing any underlying conditions is also crucial.

Prognosis: With appropriate treatment, the prognosis for cats with gastric ulcers is generally good. However, complications such as perforation or bleeding can lead to more serious outcomes.

3. Gastric Foreign Bodies

Etiology: Foreign bodies in the stomach can include ingested toys, bones, or other objects. These can cause obstruction or irritation of the stomach lining.

Diagnosis: Clinical signs such as vomiting, anorexia, and abdominal pain may suggest a foreign body. Imaging studies, such as X-rays or ultrasound, are used to confirm the presence of the object.

Treatment: Treatment typically involves surgical removal of the foreign body. Supportive care, including fluid therapy and pain management, is also important.

Prognosis: The prognosis for cats with gastric foreign bodies is generally good with prompt treatment. However, delays in treatment can lead to complications such as perforation or peritonitis.

4. Hairballs (Trichobezoars)

Etiology: Hairballs form when ingested hair accumulates in the stomach and fails to pass through the digestive tract. While grooming is a normal behavior, excessive grooming or shedding can increase the risk of hairball formation.

Diagnosis: Hairballs are often diagnosed based on clinical history and the presence of cylindrical hair masses in vomit. Imaging studies may be used if an obstruction is suspected.

Treatment: Treatment focuses on preventing hairball formation through regular grooming, dietary management, and the use of hairball remedies. In cases of obstruction, surgical intervention may be necessary.

Prognosis: The prognosis for cats with hairballs is generally good with appropriate management. However, recurrent hairballs may indicate underlying skin or gastrointestinal issues that require further investigation.

5. Gastric Neoplasia

Etiology: Gastric neoplasia, or stomach cancer, is relatively rare in cats. Lymphoma is the most common type, but other tumors such as adenocarcinomas can also occur. The exact cause of gastric neoplasia is often unknown, but genetic and environmental factors may play a role.

Diagnosis: Diagnosis involves a combination of imaging studies, endoscopy, and biopsy. Blood tests may also be used to assess the cat's overall health and organ function.

Treatment: Treatment depends on the type and stage of the tumor. Options may include surgery, chemotherapy, and supportive care.

Prognosis: The prognosis for cats with gastric neoplasia varies depending on the type and extent of the tumor. Early detection and treatment can improve outcomes, but the overall prognosis is often guarded.

Stomach-related digestive issues in cats can range from relatively benign conditions like hairballs to more serious problems such as gastric neoplasia. Prompt recognition and appropriate veterinary care are essential for managing these conditions and ensuring the best possible outcomes for our feline patients. Regular check-ups and attention to changes in eating behavior and overall health can help catch these issues early, providing a better quality of life for our beloved cats.

The Small Intestine

The small intestine plays a crucial role in the digestion and absorption of nutrients. In cats, several conditions can affect this vital organ, leading to a range of symptoms and potential complications.

1. Inflammatory Bowel Disease (IBD)

Etiology: IBD is a group of disorders characterized by chronic inflammation of the gastrointestinal tract. The exact cause is unknown, but it is believed to involve a combination of genetic, immunologic, and environmental factors.

Diagnosis: Diagnosis typically involves a combination of clinical signs, blood tests, imaging studies, and intestinal biopsies obtained via endoscopy or exploratory surgery.

Treatment: Treatment aims to reduce inflammation and manage symptoms. This may include dietary changes, such as hypoallergenic or high-fiber diets, and medications like corticosteroids and immunosuppressants.

Prognosis: The prognosis for cats with IBD varies depending on the severity and response to treatment. With appropriate management, many cats can achieve good long-term control of their symptoms.

2. Intestinal Parasites

Etiology: Common intestinal parasites in cats include roundworms, hookworms, and tapeworms. Infection can occur through ingestion of infected prey, contaminated soil, or flea infestation.

Diagnosis: Diagnosis is typically made through fecal examinations to identify parasite eggs or segments.

Treatment: Treatment involves the administration of anthelmintic medications to eliminate the parasites. Regular deworming and flea control are also important preventive measures.

Prognosis: With prompt treatment, the prognosis for cats with intestinal parasites is generally excellent.

3. Intestinal Obstructions

Etiology: Obstructions can be caused by ingested foreign objects, tumors, strictures, or intussusception (telescoping of one part of the intestine into another).

Diagnosis: Clinical signs such as vomiting, anorexia, and abdominal pain may suggest an obstruction. Imaging studies, such as X-rays or ultrasound, are used to confirm the diagnosis.

Treatment: Treatment typically involves surgical removal of the obstruction. Supportive care, including fluid therapy and pain management, is also important.

Prognosis: The prognosis for cats with intestinal obstructions is generally good with prompt surgical intervention. However, delays in treatment can lead to complications such as perforation or peritonitis.

4. Enteritis

Etiology: Enteritis is the inflammation of the small intestine, which can be caused by infections (bacterial, viral, or parasitic), dietary indiscretions, or inflammatory conditions like IBD.

Diagnosis: Diagnosis is based on clinical signs and may be supported by blood tests, fecal examinations, and imaging studies. Endoscopy and biopsies may be necessary for definitive diagnosis.

Treatment: Treatment focuses on addressing the underlying cause and providing supportive care. This may include antibiotics for bacterial infections, dietary management, and anti-inflammatory medications.

Prognosis: The prognosis for cats with enteritis varies depending on the cause and severity of the condition. With appropriate treatment, many cases can be managed successfully.

5. Small Intestinal Bacterial Overgrowth (SIBO)

Etiology: SIBO occurs when there is an abnormal increase in the population of bacteria in the small intestine. It can be associated with conditions that disrupt normal intestinal motility or the immune system.

Diagnosis: Diagnosis can be challenging and may involve a combination of clinical signs, blood tests, and specialized tests to assess bacterial populations.

Treatment: Treatment typically involves antibiotics to reduce the bacterial overgrowth and dietary modifications to support intestinal health.

Prognosis: With appropriate treatment, the prognosis for cats with SIBO is generally good. However, addressing any underlying conditions is crucial for long-term management.

6. Intestinal Lymphoma

Etiology: Intestinal lymphoma is a type of cancer that affects the lymphocytes in the small intestine. It is the most common form of gastrointestinal cancer in cats and may be associated with feline leukemia virus (FeLV) or feline immunodeficiency virus (FIV) infection.

Diagnosis: Diagnosis involves imaging studies, endoscopy, and biopsies to confirm the presence of cancerous cells.

Treatment: Treatment options include chemotherapy, surgery, and supportive care. The choice of treatment depends on the stage and type of lymphoma.

Prognosis: The prognosis for cats with intestinal lymphoma varies depending on the stage and response to treatment. Early detection and aggressive treatment can improve outcomes.

Small intestine-related digestive issues in cats can range from relatively benign conditions like intestinal parasites to more serious diseases such as intestinal lymphoma. Early recognition and appropriate veterinary care are essential for managing these conditions and ensuring the best possible outcomes for our feline patients. Regular check-ups and attention to changes in eating behavior, stool consistency, and overall health can help catch these issues early, providing a better quality of life for our beloved cats.

The Large Intestine

The large intestine, or colon, plays a crucial role in the final stages of digestion, including water absorption and feces formation. In cats, several conditions can affect the large intestine, leading to a range of symptoms and potential complications.

1. Colitis

Etiology: Colitis is the inflammation of the colon. It can be acute or chronic and is often caused by infections (bacterial, viral, or parasitic), dietary indiscretions, inflammatory bowel disease (IBD), or stress.

Diagnosis: Diagnosis typically involves a combination of clinical signs, fecal examinations, blood tests, and imaging studies. Colonoscopy and biopsies may be necessary for a definitive diagnosis.

Treatment: Treatment focuses on addressing the underlying cause and providing symptomatic relief. This may include dietary changes, such as a high-fiber or hypoallergenic diet, and medications like anti-inflammatories, antibiotics, or probiotics.

Prognosis: The prognosis for cats with colitis varies depending on the cause and severity. Acute colitis often resolves with appropriate treatment, while chronic colitis may require ongoing management.

2. Constipation

Etiology: Constipation is the infrequent or difficult passage of stool. It can be caused by dehydration, dietary factors, lack of exercise, obesity, or underlying medical conditions such as megacolon or pelvic injuries.

Diagnosis: Diagnosis is based on clinical signs and physical examination. Imaging studies, such as X-rays or ultrasound, can help assess the severity and identify any underlying causes.

Treatment: Treatment aims to relieve constipation and address any contributing factors. This may include dietary changes, such as increased fiber or moisture content, laxatives, stool softeners, and, in severe cases, enemas or manual evacuation under anesthesia.

Prognosis: The prognosis for cats with constipation is generally good with appropriate treatment. However, chronic or recurrent constipation may require long-term management.

3. Megacolon

Etiology: Megacolon is characterized by the abnormal dilation and decreased motility of the colon. It can be congenital or acquired, with the latter often being a result of chronic constipation.

Diagnosis: Diagnosis involves imaging studies, such as X-rays or ultrasound, which reveal an enlarged colon. A thorough medical history and physical examination are also important to rule out other causes of constipation.

Treatment: Treatment focuses on relieving constipation and maintaining regular bowel movements. This may include dietary changes, medications to promote colonic motility, and, in severe cases, surgery to remove the affected portion of the colon.

Prognosis: The prognosis for cats with megacolon varies depending on the severity and response to treatment. Early intervention and consistent management are crucial for a positive outcome.

4. Feline Irritable Bowel Syndrome (IBS)

Etiology: IBS is a functional disorder characterized by chronic abdominal pain and altered bowel habits. It is believed to be caused by a combination of stress, dietary factors, and abnormal gut motility.

Diagnosis: IBS is a diagnosis of exclusion, made after ruling out other gastrointestinal conditions. A thorough medical history, physical examination, and diagnostic tests are necessary to eliminate other potential causes.

Treatment: Treatment aims to manage symptoms and may include dietary modifications, stress reduction, and medications to regulate gut motility.

Prognosis: The prognosis for cats with IBS is generally good with appropriate management. However, it may require ongoing adjustments to treatment and lifestyle to maintain symptom control.

5. Colonic Neoplasia

Etiology: Colonic neoplasia refers to tumors of the colon, which can be benign (polyps) or malignant (adenocarcinomas). The exact cause is often unknown, but genetic and environmental factors may play a role.

Diagnosis: Diagnosis involves imaging studies and endoscopy, with biopsies taken to confirm the presence of cancerous cells.

Treatment: Treatment depends on the type and stage of the tumor. Surgical removal is the primary treatment for localized tumors, while advanced cases may require chemotherapy or radiation therapy.

Prognosis: The prognosis for cats with colonic neoplasia varies depending on the type and extent of the tumor. Early detection and treatment can improve outcomes, but the overall prognosis is often guarded.

Large intestine-related digestive issues in cats can significantly impact their quality of life and overall health. Early recognition and appropriate veterinary care are essential for managing these conditions and ensuring the best possible outcomes for our feline patients. Regular check-ups and attention to changes in bowel habits, stool consistency, and overall well-being can help catch these issues early, providing a better quality of life for our beloved cats.

The Rectum and Anus

The rectum and anus are integral parts of the digestive system, playing a crucial role in the expulsion of feces. In cats, several conditions can affect these areas, leading to discomfort and potential health problems.

1. Anal Gland Impaction

Etiology: Anal glands are two small sacs located on either side of the anus. They produce a secretion that is normally expelled during defecation. Impaction occurs when the glands become blocked, leading to the accumulation of secretions.

Diagnosis: Signs of anal gland impaction include scooting, licking the anal area, and discomfort during defecation. Physical examination by a veterinarian can confirm the impaction.

Treatment: Treatment involves manually expressing the impacted glands to relieve the blockage. In recurrent cases, dietary changes, regular gland expression, or surgical removal of the glands may be considered.

Prognosis: The prognosis for cats with anal gland impaction is generally good with appropriate treatment. However, some cats may experience recurrent episodes.

2. Anal Gland Abscess

Etiology: An anal gland abscess occurs when an impacted gland becomes infected, leading to the formation of an abscess. It can be caused by bacteria or foreign material entering the gland.

Diagnosis: Symptoms include severe pain, swelling near the anus, fever, and lethargy. A physical examination and possibly imaging studies can confirm the presence of an abscess.

Treatment: Treatment involves draining the abscess, either through manual expression or surgery, and administering antibiotics to treat the infection. Pain management is also important.

Prognosis: With prompt treatment, the prognosis for cats with anal gland abscesses is generally good. However, there is a risk of recurrence if the underlying cause is not addressed.

3. Constipation and Obstipation

Etiology: Constipation is the infrequent or difficult passage of stool, while obstipation is a severe form of constipation where defecation is impossible. Causes include dehydration, dietary factors, lack of exercise, or underlying medical conditions.

Diagnosis: Diagnosis is based on clinical signs and a physical examination. Imaging studies, such as X-rays, can help assess the severity and identify any underlying causes.

Treatment: Treatment aims to relieve constipation and address any contributing factors. This may include dietary changes, laxatives, enemas, and, in severe cases, manual removal of feces under anesthesia.

Prognosis: The prognosis for cats with constipation is generally good with appropriate treatment. However, obstipation can be more challenging to manage and may require long-term dietary and medical management.

4. Perianal Fistulas

Etiology: Perianal fistulas are abnormal openings around the anus that can result from infections, trauma, or inflammatory conditions.

Diagnosis: Symptoms include pain, discharge, and swelling around the anus. Diagnosis is typically made through physical examination and imaging studies.

Treatment: Treatment depends on the severity and underlying cause. It may include antibiotics, anti-inflammatory medications, and, in some cases, surgical intervention to remove the fistulas.

Prognosis: The prognosis for cats with perianal fistulas varies depending on the cause and response to treatment. Early intervention and appropriate management can improve outcomes.

5. Rectal Prolapse

Etiology: Rectal prolapse occurs when part of the rectum protrudes through the anus. It can be caused by straining during defecation, intestinal parasites, or other underlying conditions that increase abdominal pressure.

Diagnosis: Rectal prolapse is easily recognizable by the protrusion of rectal tissue from the anus. A thorough examination is necessary to determine the extent and underlying cause.

Treatment: Treatment involves addressing the underlying cause and may include manual reduction of the prolapse, surgery to repair the prolapse, and supportive care.

Prognosis: The prognosis for cats with rectal prolapse varies depending on the underlying cause and the severity of the prolapse. With appropriate treatment, many cats can make a full recovery.

6. Anal Sac Adenocarcinoma

Etiology: Anal sac adenocarcinoma is a malignant tumor of the anal glands. The exact cause is unknown, but older cats are more commonly affected.

Diagnosis: Symptoms may include a palpable mass near the anus, difficulty defecating, and signs of systemic illness. Diagnosis is confirmed through biopsy and imaging studies to assess the extent of the disease.

Treatment: Treatment options include surgical removal of the tumor, radiation therapy, and chemotherapy. The choice of treatment depends on the stage of the cancer and the overall health of the cat.

Prognosis: The prognosis for cats with anal sac adenocarcinoma varies depending on the stage of the cancer and the response to treatment. Early detection and aggressive treatment can improve outcomes.

Rectum and anus-related digestive issues in cats can range from relatively minor conditions like anal gland impaction to more serious problems such as anal sac adenocarcinoma. Prompt recognition and appropriate veterinary care are essential for managing these conditions and ensuring the best possible outcomes for our feline patients. Regular check-ups and attention to changes in defecation habits and anal area health can help catch these issues early, providing a better quality of life for our beloved cats.

****

Chapter 4

Digestive Medical Conditions, Diseases, and Illnesses Common to Dogs

The Mouth

The mouth is the gateway to the digestive system, and various conditions can affect this crucial area in dogs. This chapter will explore the most common digestive issues in dogs, including their causes, diagnosis, treatment, and prognosis.

1. Periodontal Disease

Etiology: Periodontal disease is the most prevalent dental issue in dogs, caused by the accumulation of plaque and tartar on the teeth. Bacteria in the plaque can infect the gums and the structures supporting the teeth, leading to inflammation, tooth loss, and systemic health issues.

Diagnosis: A thorough oral examination, often under anesthesia, is required to diagnose periodontal disease. Dental radiographs may be necessary to assess the extent of the disease.

Treatment: Treatment involves professional dental cleaning to remove plaque and tartar, followed by regular home dental care. In advanced cases, extraction of affected teeth may be necessary.

Prognosis: With early detection and proper treatment, the prognosis for dogs with periodontal disease is generally good. However, ongoing dental care is essential to prevent recurrence.

2. Stomatitis

Etiology: Stomatitis is a severe, painful inflammation of the mouth and gums. Its exact cause is unknown, but it is believed to be an immune-mediated response to plaque or other oral antigens.

Diagnosis: Diagnosis is based on clinical signs and oral examination. Biopsies may be performed to rule out other conditions.

Treatment: Treatment often involves extensive dental extractions to remove sources of inflammation. Anti-inflammatory medications and pain management are also important. In some cases, immunosuppressive drugs may be used.

Prognosis: Stomatitis can be challenging to manage, and long-term treatment may be necessary. The prognosis varies, with some dogs responding well to treatment and others requiring ongoing care.

3. Tooth Fractures

Etiology: Tooth fractures in dogs can result from trauma, chewing on hard objects, or underlying dental disease. The pulp of the tooth may be exposed, leading to pain and infection.

Diagnosis: Fractured teeth can often be identified through a visual examination. Dental radiographs may be needed to assess the extent of the damage and any associated pulp exposure.

Treatment: Treatment depends on the severity of the fracture. Options may include root canal therapy, vital pulp therapy, or extraction of the affected tooth.

Prognosis: The prognosis for dogs with tooth fractures is generally good with appropriate treatment. However, timely intervention is crucial to prevent complications such as infection or abscess formation.

4. Oral Tumors

Etiology: Oral tumors in dogs can be benign or malignant, with squamous cell carcinoma and melanoma being the most common malignant tumors. Risk factors may include genetics, environmental factors, and certain viruses.

Diagnosis: Diagnosis involves a thorough oral examination and biopsy of the tumor. Imaging studies may be needed to assess the extent of the disease.

Treatment: Treatment depends on the type and location of the tumor. Surgery, radiation therapy, and chemotherapy may be options.

Prognosis: The prognosis for dogs with oral tumors varies widely depending on the type and stage of the tumor. Early detection and treatment are crucial for a better outcome.

5. Gingivitis

Etiology: Gingivitis is the inflammation of the gums, often caused by the accumulation of plaque and tartar. It can also be associated with systemic diseases such as diabetes or kidney disease.

Diagnosis: A visual examination of the gums can reveal redness, swelling, and bleeding, indicating gingivitis. Further tests may be required to diagnose underlying systemic conditions.

Treatment: Treatment involves professional dental cleaning to remove plaque and tartar, followed by regular home dental care. Addressing any underlying systemic conditions is also important.

Prognosis: With proper treatment and ongoing dental care, the prognosis for dogs with gingivitis is generally good. However, without proper care, it can progress to more severe periodontal disease.

6. Oral Papillomas

Etiology: Oral papillomas are warts caused by the canine papillomavirus. They typically affect young dogs and are transmitted through direct contact with infected dogs or contaminated objects.

Diagnosis: Oral papillomas are usually diagnosed based on their characteristic appearance. Biopsy may be performed to confirm the diagnosis.

Treatment: In most cases, oral papillomas will regress spontaneously within a few months. In severe cases, surgical removal or other treatments may be necessary.

Prognosis: The prognosis for dogs with oral papillomas is generally excellent, as the condition is usually self-limiting. However, it is important to monitor the lesions and seek veterinary care if they do not resolve or if complications arise.

Mouth-related digestive issues in dogs can range from common conditions like periodontal disease and gingivitis to more serious problems such as oral tumors. Early detection and appropriate treatment are key to managing these conditions and ensuring the overall well-being of our canine companions. Regular veterinary check-ups, including dental examinations, are essential for maintaining optimal oral health in dogs. As dog owners, it's crucial to be vigilant about your pet's oral hygiene and seek veterinary care at the first sign of any dental problems.

The Esophagus

The esophagus is a critical component of the canine digestive system, responsible for transporting food from the mouth to the stomach. Various conditions can affect the esophagus in dogs, leading to a range of symptoms and potential complications. In this section we will explore the most common esophagus-related digestive issues in dogs, including their causes, diagnosis, treatment, and prognosis.

1. Esophagitis

Etiology: Esophagitis is the inflammation of the esophagus, often caused by acid reflux, foreign body ingestion, or anesthesia-related complications. It can also result from infections or certain medications.

Diagnosis: Diagnosis typically involves endoscopy, which allows direct visualization of the esophageal lining. Biopsies may be taken to assess the extent of inflammation and rule out other conditions.

Treatment: Treatment focuses on addressing the underlying cause, managing symptoms, and protecting the esophageal lining. This may include antacids, gastroprotectants, and anti-inflammatory medications. Dietary management, such as feeding a bland, easily digestible diet, can also be beneficial.

Prognosis: The prognosis for dogs with esophagitis is generally good if the underlying cause is identified and appropriately managed. However, chronic or severe cases may lead to complications such as strictures.

2. Esophageal Obstruction

Etiology: Esophageal obstruction, or foreign body impaction, occurs when an object becomes lodged in the esophagus. Common culprits include bones, toys, or food boluses. Dogs with esophageal strictures or motility disorders are at higher risk for obstructions.

Diagnosis: Clinical signs such as regurgitation, drooling, and distress are suggestive of an obstruction. Imaging studies, such as X-rays or endoscopy, are used to confirm the diagnosis and locate the obstruction.

Treatment: Treatment involves the removal of the foreign object, which may be achieved through endoscopy or, in some cases, surgery. Supportive care, including hydration and pain management, is also important.

Prognosis: With prompt treatment, the prognosis for dogs with esophageal obstructions is generally good. However, delays in treatment or complications can lead to more serious outcomes.

3. Esophageal Strictures

Etiology: Esophageal strictures are the narrowing of the esophagus, often resulting from chronic inflammation, injury, or acid reflux. They can lead to difficulty swallowing and regurgitation.

Diagnosis: Strictures can be diagnosed using endoscopy or contrast radiography, which allows visualization of the narrowed area.

Treatment: Treatment often involves esophageal dilation, a procedure to stretch the narrowed area. This may need to be repeated multiple times. Medications to reduce acid reflux and inflammation may also be prescribed.

Prognosis: The prognosis for dogs with esophageal strictures varies depending on the severity and response to treatment. In some cases, strictures can recur, requiring ongoing management.

4. Megaesophagus

Etiology: Megaesophagus is characterized by the dilation and decreased motility of the esophagus. It can be congenital or acquired, with potential causes including neuromuscular disorders, infections, or idiopathic (unknown) factors.

Diagnosis: Clinical signs such as regurgitation and weight loss, along with radiographic evidence of an enlarged esophagus, support the diagnosis of megaesophagus.

Treatment: Treatment focuses on managing symptoms and addressing any underlying causes. Feeding modifications, such as offering small, frequent meals from an elevated position, can help reduce regurgitation.

Prognosis: The prognosis for dogs with megaesophagus varies depending on the underlying cause and the severity of the condition. In some cases, it can be managed effectively with dietary and lifestyle changes.

5. Gastroesophageal Reflux Disease (GERD)

Etiology: GERD occurs when stomach acid flows back into the esophagus, causing irritation and inflammation. It can be triggered by factors such as anesthesia, obesity, or hiatal hernias.

Diagnosis: Diagnosis is often based on clinical signs and response to treatment. Endoscopy may be used to assess the extent of esophageal damage.

Treatment: Treatment includes dietary management, such as feeding smaller, more frequent meals, and medications to reduce stomach acid and protect the esophageal lining.

Prognosis: With appropriate treatment, the prognosis for dogs with GERD is generally good. However, long-term management may be necessary to prevent recurrence.

6. Esophageal Tumors

Etiology: Esophageal tumors are relatively rare in dogs. They can be benign or malignant, with squamous cell carcinoma being the most common type of malignant tumor.

Diagnosis: Symptoms may include difficulty swallowing, regurgitation, and weight loss. Diagnosis is confirmed through endoscopy, biopsy, and imaging studies to assess the extent of the tumor.

Treatment: Treatment options vary depending on the type and location of the tumor. Surgery, radiation therapy, and chemotherapy may be considered.

Prognosis: The prognosis for dogs with esophageal tumors is generally guarded, as these tumors are often aggressive and difficult to treat. Early detection and intervention can improve outcomes.

Esophagus-related digestive issues in dogs can range from mild conditions like esophagitis to more serious problems such as esophageal tumors. Early recognition and appropriate veterinary care are essential for managing these conditions and ensuring the best possible outcomes for our canine patients. Regular check-ups and attention to changes in eating behavior can help catch these issues early, providing a better quality of life for our beloved dogs.

The Stomach

The stomach is a key player in the digestive system, responsible for the initial breakdown of food. In dogs, various conditions can affect the stomach, leading to a range of symptoms and potential complications.

1. Gastritis

Etiology: Gastritis refers to the inflammation of the stomach lining. It can be acute or chronic and is often caused by dietary indiscretion, infections, toxins, or stress. Chronic gastritis may also be associated with underlying health conditions, such as kidney disease or inflammatory bowel disease (IBD).

Diagnosis: Diagnosis typically involves a combination of clinical signs, blood tests, imaging studies, and intestinal biopsies obtained via endoscopy or exploratory surgery.

Treatment: Treatment aims to reduce inflammation and manage symptoms. This may include dietary changes, such as hypoallergenic or high-fiber diets, and medications like corticosteroids and immunosuppressants.

Prognosis: The prognosis for dogs with gastritis varies depending on the severity and response to treatment. With appropriate management, many dogs can achieve good long-term control of their symptoms.

2. Gastric Ulcers

Etiology: Gastric ulcers are lesions that form in the stomach lining. They can be caused by prolonged use of nonsteroidal anti-inflammatory drugs (NSAIDs), stress, infections, or underlying diseases that increase stomach acidity.

Diagnosis: Ulcers are diagnosed through endoscopy, which allows for direct visualization of the lesions. Blood tests and imaging studies may also be used to assess the dog's overall health and identify any contributing factors.

Treatment: Treatment aims to reduce stomach acid and protect the ulcerated area. This may include proton pump inhibitors, H2 receptor antagonists, and sucralfate. Addressing any underlying conditions is also crucial.

Prognosis: With appropriate treatment, the prognosis for dogs with gastric ulcers is generally good. However, complications such as perforation or bleeding can lead to more serious outcomes.

3. Gastric Dilatation-Volvulus (GDV)

Etiology: GDV, also known as bloat, is a life-threatening condition where the stomach becomes distended with gas and then twists on itself. It is more common in large, deep-chested breeds. The exact cause is unknown, but factors such as eating large meals quickly, exercise after eating, and stress may contribute.

Diagnosis: GDV is a medical emergency requiring immediate veterinary attention. Diagnosis is typically made based on clinical signs, physical examination, and imaging studies, such as X-rays.

Treatment: Treatment involves stabilizing the dog, decompressing the stomach, and then surgical intervention to untwist the stomach and secure it in place to prevent recurrence (gastropexy).

Prognosis: The prognosis for dogs with GDV depends on the severity and timing of treatment. With prompt intervention, many dogs can recover, but the condition can be fatal if not treated quickly.

4. Gastric Foreign Bodies

Etiology: Foreign bodies in the stomach can include ingested toys, bones, or other objects. These can cause obstruction or irritation of the stomach lining.

Diagnosis: Clinical signs such as vomiting, anorexia, and abdominal pain may suggest a foreign body. Imaging studies, such as X-rays or ultrasound, are used to confirm the presence of the object.

Treatment: Treatment typically involves surgical removal of the foreign body. Supportive care, including fluid therapy and pain management, is also important.

Prognosis: The prognosis for dogs with gastric foreign bodies is generally good with prompt treatment. However, delays in treatment can lead to complications such as perforation or peritonitis.

5. Chronic Enteropathy

Etiology: Chronic enteropathy is a term used to describe a group of disorders characterized by chronic gastrointestinal symptoms, such as vomiting and diarrhea. The exact cause is often unknown, but it may be related to food sensitivities, immune-mediated diseases, or infections.

Diagnosis: Diagnosis involves a combination of clinical signs, blood tests, imaging studies, and intestinal biopsies.

Treatment: Treatment depends on the underlying cause and may include dietary changes, such as hypoallergenic diets, medications to control inflammation, and antibiotics for bacterial overgrowth.

Prognosis: The prognosis for dogs with chronic enteropathy varies depending on the underlying cause and response to treatment. Many dogs can achieve good long-term control of their symptoms with appropriate management.

6. Gastric Neoplasia

Etiology: Gastric neoplasia refers to tumors of the stomach, which can be benign (polyps) or malignant (adenocarcinomas). The exact cause is often unknown, but genetic and environmental factors may play a role.

Diagnosis: Diagnosis involves imaging studies and endoscopy, with biopsies taken to confirm the presence of cancerous cells.

Treatment: Treatment depends on the type and stage of the tumor. Surgical removal is the primary treatment for localized tumors, while advanced cases may require chemotherapy or radiation therapy.

Prognosis: The prognosis for dogs with gastric neoplasia varies depending on the type and extent of the tumor. Early detection and treatment can improve outcomes, but the overall prognosis is often guarded.

Stomach-related digestive issues in dogs can range from relatively benign conditions like gastritis to more serious problems such as gastric neoplasia. Early recognition and appropriate veterinary care are essential for managing these conditions and ensuring the best possible outcomes for our canine patients. Regular check-ups and attention to changes in eating behavior and overall health can help catch these issues early, providing a better quality of life for our beloved dogs.

The Small Intestine

The small intestine is a crucial component of the canine digestive system, responsible for the majority of nutrient absorption. Several conditions can affect the small intestine in dogs, leading to various symptoms and potential complications.

1. Inflammatory Bowel Disease (IBD)

Etiology: IBD is a group of disorders characterized by chronic inflammation of the gastrointestinal tract. The exact cause is unknown, but it is believed to involve a combination of genetic, immunologic, and environmental factors.

Diagnosis: Diagnosis typically involves a combination of clinical signs, blood tests, imaging studies, and intestinal biopsies obtained via endoscopy or exploratory surgery.

Treatment: Treatment aims to reduce inflammation and manage symptoms. This may include dietary changes, such as hypoallergenic or high-fiber diets, and medications like corticosteroids and immunosuppressants.

Prognosis: The prognosis for dogs with IBD varies depending on the severity and response to treatment. With appropriate management, many dogs can achieve good long-term control of their symptoms.

2. Intestinal Parasites

Etiology: Common intestinal parasites in dogs include roundworms, hookworms, whipworms, and tapeworms. Infection can occur through ingestion of infected soil, feces, or prey.

Diagnosis: Diagnosis is typically made through fecal examinations to identify parasite eggs or segments.

Treatment: Treatment involves the administration of anthelmintic medications to eliminate the parasites. Regular deworming and hygiene measures are also important preventive measures.

Prognosis: With prompt treatment, the prognosis for dogs with intestinal parasites is generally excellent.

3. Intestinal Obstructions

Etiology: Obstructions can be caused by ingested foreign objects, tumors, strictures, or intussusception (telescoping of one part of the intestine into another).

Diagnosis: Clinical signs such as vomiting, anorexia, and abdominal pain may suggest an obstruction. Imaging studies, such as X-rays or ultrasound, are used to confirm the diagnosis.

Treatment: Treatment typically involves surgical removal of the obstruction. Supportive care, including fluid therapy and pain management, is also important.

Prognosis: The prognosis for dogs with intestinal obstructions is generally good with prompt surgical intervention. However, delays in treatment can lead to complications such as perforation or peritonitis.

4. Enteritis

Etiology: Enteritis is the inflammation of the small intestine, which can be caused by infections (bacterial, viral, or parasitic), dietary indiscretions, or inflammatory conditions like IBD.

Diagnosis: Diagnosis is based on clinical signs and may be supported by blood tests, fecal examinations, and imaging studies. Endoscopy and biopsies may be necessary for definitive diagnosis.

Treatment: Treatment focuses on addressing the underlying cause and providing supportive care. This may include antibiotics for bacterial infections, dietary management, and anti-inflammatory medications.

Prognosis: The prognosis for dogs with enteritis varies depending on the cause and severity of the condition. With appropriate treatment, many cases can be managed successfully.

5. Small Intestinal Bacterial Overgrowth (SIBO)

Etiology: SIBO occurs when there is an abnormal increase in the population of bacteria in the small intestine. It can be associated with conditions that disrupt normal intestinal motility or the immune system.

Diagnosis: Diagnosis can be challenging and may involve a combination of clinical signs, blood tests, and specialized tests to assess bacterial populations.

Treatment: Treatment typically involves antibiotics to reduce the bacterial overgrowth and dietary modifications to support intestinal health.

Prognosis: With appropriate treatment, the prognosis for dogs with SIBO is generally good. However, addressing any underlying conditions is crucial for long-term management.

6. Intestinal Lymphoma

Etiology: Intestinal lymphoma is a type of cancer that affects the lymphocytes in the small intestine. It is the most common form of gastrointestinal cancer in dogs and may be associated with chronic inflammation or immune suppression.

Diagnosis: Diagnosis involves imaging studies, endoscopy, and biopsies to confirm the presence of cancerous cells.

Treatment: Treatment options include chemotherapy, surgery, and supportive care. The choice of treatment depends on the stage and type of lymphoma.

Prognosis: The prognosis for dogs with intestinal lymphoma varies depending on the stage and response to treatment. Early detection and aggressive treatment can improve outcomes.

Small intestine-related digestive issues in dogs can range from relatively benign conditions like intestinal parasites to more serious diseases such as intestinal lymphoma. Early recognition and appropriate veterinary care are essential for managing these conditions and ensuring the best possible outcomes for our canine patients. Regular check-ups and attention to changes in eating behavior, stool consistency, and overall health can help catch these issues early, providing a better quality of life for our beloved dogs.

The Large Intestine

The large intestine, or colon, is the final part of the digestive system, playing a crucial role in water absorption and feces formation. In dogs, various conditions can affect the large intestine, leading to symptoms such as diarrhea, constipation, and discomfort.

1. Colitis

Etiology: Colitis refers to the inflammation of the colon. It can be acute or chronic and is often caused by infections (bacterial, viral, or parasitic), dietary indiscretions, inflammatory bowel disease (IBD), or stress.

Diagnosis: Diagnosis typically involves a combination of clinical signs, fecal examinations, blood tests, and imaging studies. Colonoscopy and biopsies may be necessary for a definitive diagnosis.

Treatment: Treatment focuses on addressing the underlying cause and providing symptomatic relief. This may include dietary changes, such as a high-fiber or hypoallergenic diet, and medications like anti-inflammatories, antibiotics, or probiotics.

Prognosis: The prognosis for dogs with colitis varies depending on the cause and severity. Acute colitis often resolves with appropriate treatment, while chronic colitis may require ongoing management.

2. Constipation and Obstipation

Etiology: Constipation is the infrequent or difficult passage of stool, while obstipation is a severe form of constipation where defecation is impossible. Causes include dehydration, dietary factors, lack of exercise, obesity, or underlying medical conditions such as megacolon or pelvic injuries.

Diagnosis: Diagnosis is based on clinical signs and a physical examination. Imaging studies, such as X-rays or ultrasound, can help assess the severity and identify any underlying causes.

Treatment: Treatment aims to relieve constipation and address any contributing factors. This may include dietary changes, such as increased fiber or moisture content, laxatives, stool softeners, and, in severe cases, enemas or manual evacuation under anesthesia.

Prognosis: The prognosis for dogs with constipation is generally good with appropriate treatment. However, obstipation can be more challenging to manage and may require long-term dietary and medical management.

3. Megacolon

Etiology: Megacolon is characterized by the abnormal dilation and decreased motility of the colon. It can be congenital or acquired, with the latter often being a result of chronic constipation.

Diagnosis: Diagnosis involves imaging studies, such as X-rays or ultrasound, which reveal an enlarged colon. A thorough medical history and physical examination are also important to rule out other causes of constipation.

Treatment: Treatment focuses on relieving constipation and maintaining regular bowel movements. This may include dietary changes, medications to promote colonic motility, and, in severe cases, surgery to remove the affected portion of the colon.

Prognosis: The prognosis for dogs with megacolon varies depending on the severity and response to treatment. Early intervention and consistent management are crucial for a positive outcome.

4. Irritable Bowel Syndrome (IBS)

Etiology: IBS is a functional disorder characterized by chronic abdominal pain and altered bowel habits. It is believed to be caused by a combination of stress, dietary factors, and abnormal gut motility.

Diagnosis: IBS is a diagnosis of exclusion, made after ruling out other gastrointestinal conditions. A thorough medical history, physical examination, and diagnostic tests are necessary to eliminate other potential causes.

Treatment: Treatment aims to manage symptoms and may include dietary modifications, stress reduction, and medications to regulate gut motility.

Prognosis: The prognosis for dogs with IBS is generally good with appropriate management. However, it may require ongoing adjustments to treatment and lifestyle to maintain symptom control.

5. Colonic Neoplasia

Etiology: Colonic neoplasia refers to tumors of the colon, which can be benign (polyps) or malignant (adenocarcinomas). The exact cause is often unknown, but genetic and environmental factors may play a role.

Diagnosis: Diagnosis involves imaging studies and endoscopy, with biopsies taken to confirm the presence of cancerous cells.

Treatment: Treatment depends on the type and stage of the tumor. Surgical removal is the primary treatment for localized tumors, while advanced cases may require chemotherapy or radiation therapy.

Prognosis: The prognosis for dogs with colonic neoplasia varies depending on the type and extent of the tumor. Early detection and treatment can improve outcomes, but the overall prognosis is often guarded.

Large intestine-related digestive issues in dogs can significantly impact their quality of life and overall health. Early recognition and appropriate veterinary care are essential for managing these conditions and ensuring the best possible outcomes for our canine patients. Regular check-ups and attention to changes in bowel habits, stool consistency, and overall well-being can help catch these issues early, providing a better quality of life for our dogs.

The Rectum and Anus

The rectum and anus are integral parts of the digestive system, playing a crucial role in the expulsion of feces. In dogs, several conditions can affect these areas, leading to discomfort and potential health problems.

1. Anal Gland Impaction

Etiology: Anal glands are two small sacs located on either side of the anus. They produce a secretion that is normally expelled during defecation. Impaction occurs when the glands become blocked, leading to the accumulation of secretions.

Diagnosis: Signs of anal gland impaction include scooting, licking the anal area, and discomfort during defecation. Physical examination by a veterinarian can confirm the impaction.

Treatment: Treatment involves manually expressing the impacted glands to relieve the blockage. In recurrent cases, dietary changes, regular gland expression, or surgical removal of the glands may be considered.

Prognosis: The prognosis for dogs with anal gland impaction is generally good with appropriate treatment. However, some dogs may experience recurrent episodes.

2. Anal Gland Abscess

Etiology: An anal gland abscess occurs when an impacted gland becomes infected, leading to the formation of an abscess. It can be caused by bacteria or foreign material entering the gland.

Diagnosis: Symptoms include severe pain, swelling near the anus, fever, and lethargy. A physical examination and possibly imaging studies can confirm the presence of an abscess.

Treatment: Treatment involves draining the abscess, either through manual expression or surgery, and administering antibiotics to treat the infection. Pain management is also important.

Prognosis: With prompt treatment, the prognosis for dogs with anal gland abscesses is generally good. However, there is a risk of recurrence if the underlying cause is not addressed.

3. Constipation and Obstipation

Etiology: Constipation is the infrequent or difficult passage of stool, while obstipation is a severe form of constipation where defecation is impossible. Causes include dehydration, dietary factors, lack of exercise, obesity, or underlying medical conditions such as megacolon or pelvic injuries.

Diagnosis: Diagnosis is based on clinical signs and a physical examination. Imaging studies, such as X-rays or ultrasound, can help assess the severity and identify any underlying causes.

Treatment: Treatment aims to relieve constipation and address any contributing factors. This may include dietary changes, such as increased fiber or moisture content, laxatives, stool softeners, and, in severe cases, enemas or manual evacuation under anesthesia.

Prognosis: The prognosis for dogs with constipation is generally good with appropriate treatment. However, obstipation can be more challenging to manage and may require long-term dietary and medical management.

4. Perianal Fistulas

Etiology: Perianal fistulas are abnormal openings around the anus that can result from infections, trauma, or inflammatory conditions.

Diagnosis: Symptoms include pain, discharge, and swelling around the anus. Diagnosis is typically made through physical examination and imaging studies.

Treatment: Treatment depends on the severity and underlying cause. It may include antibiotics, anti-inflammatory medications, and, in some cases, surgical intervention to remove the fistulas.

Prognosis: The prognosis for dogs with perianal fistulas varies depending on the cause and response to treatment. Early intervention and appropriate management can improve outcomes.

5. Rectal Prolapse

Etiology: Rectal prolapse occurs when part of the rectum protrudes through the anus. It can be caused by straining during defecation, intestinal parasites, or other underlying conditions that increase abdominal pressure.

Diagnosis: Rectal prolapse is easily recognizable by the protrusion of rectal tissue from the anus. A thorough examination is necessary to determine the extent and underlying cause.

Treatment: Treatment involves addressing the underlying cause and may include manual reduction of the prolapse, surgery to repair the prolapse, and supportive care.

Prognosis: The prognosis for dogs with rectal prolapse varies depending on the underlying cause and the severity of the prolapse. With appropriate treatment, many dogs can make a full recovery.

6. Anal Sac Adenocarcinoma

Etiology: Anal sac adenocarcinoma is a malignant tumor of the anal glands. The exact cause is unknown, but older dogs are more commonly affected.

Diagnosis: Symptoms may include a palpable mass near the anus, difficulty defecating, and signs of systemic illness. Diagnosis is confirmed through biopsy and imaging studies to assess the extent of the disease.

Treatment: Treatment options include surgical removal of the tumor, radiation therapy, and chemotherapy. The choice of treatment depends on the stage of the cancer and the overall health of the dog.

Prognosis: The prognosis for dogs with anal sac adenocarcinoma varies depending on the stage of the cancer and the response to treatment. Early detection and aggressive treatment can improve outcomes.

Rectum and anus-related digestive issues in dogs can range from relatively minor conditions like anal gland impaction to more serious problems such as anal sac adenocarcinoma. Prompt recognition and appropriate veterinary care are essential for managing these conditions and ensuring the best possible outcomes for our canine patients.

****

Chapter 5

The Importance of Balanced Nutrition in Cats and Dogs

Essential Nutrients for Optimal Health in Cats and Dogs

Proper nutrition is the cornerstone of health for both cats and dogs. A balanced diet ensures that these animals receive the right amounts of essential nutrients to maintain overall health, support growth and development, and prevent nutritional deficiencies.

1. Proteins

Role in Health: Proteins are the building blocks of the body, essential for the growth, repair, and maintenance of tissues. They are also crucial for the proper functioning of the immune system and the production of enzymes and hormones.

Sources: High-quality animal-based proteins such as meat, poultry, fish, and eggs are excellent sources for cats and dogs. For dogs, some plant-based proteins like legumes and grains can also contribute to their protein intake.

Considerations: Cats have a higher protein requirement than dogs due to their unique metabolism. It's important to ensure that the protein sources are easily digestible and provide all the essential amino acids.

2. Fats

Role in Health: Fats are a concentrated source of energy and are vital for the absorption of fat-soluble vitamins (A, D, E, and K). They also play a role in maintaining healthy skin and coat, and supporting brain and eye health.

Sources: Animal fats from meat and fish, as well as plant-based oils like flaxseed and coconut oil, provide essential fatty acids such as omega-3 and omega-6.

Considerations: The balance between omega-3 and omega-6 fatty acids is crucial for reducing inflammation and supporting overall health. Too much fat can lead to obesity, so it's important to monitor the fat content in the diet.

3. Carbohydrates

Role in Health: While not considered essential, carbohydrates provide a readily available energy source and contribute to a healthy digestive system by providing dietary fiber.

Sources: Whole grains, vegetables, and fruits are common carbohydrate sources in pet foods. They also provide vitamins, minerals, and antioxidants.

Considerations: The carbohydrate content in the diet should be balanced, as excessive carbohydrates can contribute to obesity and other health issues. For cats, a low-carbohydrate diet is often recommended due to their carnivorous nature.

4. Vitamins

Role in Health: Vitamins are involved in a wide range of physiological processes, including immune function, bone health, and energy metabolism.

Sources: Both cats and dogs require a variety of vitamins, which can be found in animal and plant-based ingredients. For example, vitamin A is abundant in liver and fish oil, while B vitamins are found in meats and whole grains.

Considerations: Each vitamin has a specific role, and deficiencies or excesses can lead to health problems. For instance, cats require a dietary source of vitamin A, as they cannot convert beta-carotene from plants into vitamin A.

5. Minerals

Role in Health: Minerals are essential for bone and tooth health, nerve function, and the regulation of metabolic processes.

Sources: Common minerals include calcium, phosphorus, potassium, and magnesium, which are found in meat, bones, dairy products, and vegetables.

Considerations: The balance between minerals such as calcium and phosphorus is crucial for bone health. Mineral imbalances can lead to health issues, so it's important to provide a diet with the right mineral ratios.

6. Water

Role in Health: Water is vital for life, playing a role in almost every bodily function, including temperature regulation, digestion, and waste elimination.

Sources: Fresh, clean water should be available at all times. Wet foods also contribute to the water intake.

Considerations: Dehydration can lead to serious health problems, so it's essential to ensure that pets have constant access to water, especially in hot weather or after exercise.

Life Stage Nutritional Requirements for Cats and Dogs

Proper nutrition is essential for the health and well-being of cats and dogs throughout their lives. From the rapid growth phase of puppies and kittens to the more sedentary senior years, the nutritional needs of pets change significantly.

1. Puppies and Kittens

Growth and Development: During this stage, pets require higher levels of protein, fat, and calories to support rapid growth, bone development, and high energy levels.

Nutritional Requirements:

- **Protein**: Essential for building muscle, organs, and other tissues. Look for diets with high-quality animal-based proteins.
- **Fat**: Provides concentrated energy and aids in the absorption of fat-soluble vitamins.
- **Calcium and Phosphorus**: Crucial for strong bone development, with an ideal ratio of about 1.2:1 (calcium:phosphorus).
- **DHA (Docosahexaenoic Acid)**: An omega-3 fatty acid important for brain and eye development.

Feeding Practices: Puppies and kittens should be fed small, frequent meals to accommodate their small stomachs and high energy needs. Weaning onto solid food should be gradual, starting around 4-6 weeks of age.

2. Adult Dogs and Cats

Maintenance and Health: Adult pets require balanced nutrition to maintain their health, body condition, and energy levels.

Nutritional Requirements:

- **Protein**: Slightly lower levels compared to puppies and kittens, but still essential for maintaining muscle mass.
- **Fat**: Provides energy and supports healthy skin and coat. Adjust fat levels to prevent obesity.
- **Fiber**: Important for digestive health. Moderate levels of fiber can help maintain bowel regularity.
- **Vitamins and Minerals**: Ensure a balanced intake to support overall health and immune function.

Feeding Practices: Adult pets should be fed according to their size, breed, and activity level. Monitor body condition and adjust portion sizes to prevent overfeeding and obesity.

3. Senior Dogs and Cats

Aging and Health Challenges: Senior pets often face health issues such as arthritis, dental problems, and decreased organ function. Their diets should support their changing needs and help manage chronic conditions.

Nutritional Requirements:

- **Protein**: High-quality, easily digestible protein is important to maintain muscle mass and support organ function.
- **Reduced Calories**: Lower calorie intake to match decreased activity levels and prevent weight gain.
- **Omega-3 Fatty Acids**: Can help reduce inflammation and support joint health.
- **Antioxidants**: Vitamins E and C, along with other antioxidants, can help support the immune system and combat oxidative stress.

Feeding Practices: Senior pets may require smaller, more frequent meals. Consider softer textures or wet food for pets with dental issues. Regular veterinary check-ups are crucial to monitor health and adjust the diet as needed.

4. Special Considerations

Pregnant and Nursing Pets: During pregnancy and lactation, pets require increased calories, protein, and certain nutrients to support fetal development and milk production.

Working and Performance Dogs: Active working dogs have higher energy and nutrient requirements to support their physical demands.

Weight Management: Overweight pets may require calorie-restricted diets, while underweight pets may need nutrient-dense, high-calorie diets.

Understanding the nutritional needs of cats and dogs at different life stages is essential for maintaining their health and well-being. A balanced diet tailored to the specific needs of each stage can support growth, maintain optimal body condition, and address the challenges of aging. Regular consultations with a veterinarian or a pet nutritionist can ensure that dietary adjustments are made appropriately to meet the evolving needs of your pet.

Special Dietary Considerations for Digestive Health in Cats and Dogs

Diet plays a crucial role in managing digestive issues in cats and dogs. The right diet can alleviate symptoms, promote healing, and improve overall gut health. This section focuses on dietary strategies to support pets with digestive problems, emphasizing easily digestible ingredients, appropriate fiber levels, and the use of probiotics. It also addresses common food intolerances and allergies that can impact digestive health.

1. Easily Digestible Ingredients

Importance: Easily digestible ingredients are essential for pets with digestive issues as they reduce the workload on the gastrointestinal (GI) tract and facilitate nutrient absorption.

Key Ingredients:

- **High-Quality Proteins**: Lean meats like chicken, turkey, and fish are easily digestible and less likely to irritate the gut.
- **Cooked Grains**: Cooked rice, oats, and barley are gentle on the stomach and provide a source of energy.
- **Cooked Vegetables**: Well-cooked, pureed vegetables like pumpkin and sweet potatoes can provide fiber and nutrients without causing distress.

2. Appropriate Fiber Levels

Role of Fiber: Fiber is important for maintaining a healthy digestive system, but the right balance is crucial. It can help regulate bowel movements, promote healthy gut bacteria, and provide a feeling of fullness.

Types of Fiber:

- **Soluble Fiber**: Found in foods like oats, apples, and beans, soluble fiber absorbs water and forms a gel-like substance, which can help soften stools.
- **Insoluble Fiber**: Found in whole grains, vegetables, and wheat bran, insoluble fiber adds bulk to stools and helps

them pass more quickly through the digestive system.

Adjusting Fiber Levels: The amount of fiber needed can vary depending on the specific digestive issue. For example, pets with diarrhea may benefit from increased soluble fiber, while those with constipation may need more insoluble fiber.

3. Probiotics and Prebiotics

Benefits: Probiotics are beneficial bacteria that can help restore and maintain a healthy balance of gut flora. Prebiotics are non-digestible fibers that feed these beneficial bacteria.

Sources:

- **Probiotics**: Supplements or probiotic-rich foods like yogurt (for dogs) can provide beneficial bacteria.
- **Prebiotics**: Ingredients like chicory root, inulin, and certain types of fiber act as food for probiotics.

4. Addressing Food Intolerances and Allergies

Food Intolerances: Unlike allergies, food intolerances do not involve the immune system. They can cause digestive symptoms like diarrhea, vomiting, and gas. Lactose intolerance is a common example.

Food Allergies: Food allergies involve an immune response to certain proteins in food. Common allergens include beef, chicken, dairy, and wheat. Symptoms can include GI issues as well as skin problems.

Dietary Management:

- **Elimination Diet**: To identify food intolerances or allergies, a veterinarian may recommend an elimination diet, where the pet is fed a limited ingredient diet or a novel protein source.

- **Hypoallergenic Diet**: For pets with confirmed allergies, a hypoallergenic diet using hydrolyzed proteins or novel proteins can help reduce symptoms.

5. Feeding Practices for Digestive Health

Meal Frequency: Smaller, more frequent meals can help reduce the burden on the digestive system and prevent overeating.

Consistency: Sudden changes in diet can disrupt the digestive system. Any dietary changes should be made gradually over several days.

Hydration: Adequate water intake is crucial for digestion. Ensure that your pet has access to fresh, clean water at all times.

Dietary management is a key component of caring for pets with digestive issues. By focusing on easily digestible ingredients, maintaining appropriate fiber levels, incorporating probiotics and prebiotics, and addressing food intolerances and allergies, pet owners can support their pet's digestive health. It's important to work closely with a veterinarian or a pet nutritionist to develop a diet plan that meets the specific needs of your pet and monitor their response to dietary changes. With the right approach, many pets with digestive issues can enjoy a comfortable and healthy life.

The Impact of Diet on Chronic Health Conditions in Cats and Dogs

Diet plays a pivotal role in the management and prevention of chronic health conditions in cats and dogs. Nutritional imbalances or inappropriate diets can contribute to the development of conditions such as obesity, diabetes, and kidney disease. This section explores the relationship between nutrition and these chronic health issues, providing guidance on dietary management and prevention strategies.

1. Obesity

Etiology: Obesity in pets is often caused by an imbalance between energy intake and expenditure. Factors include overfeeding, lack of exercise, and consuming high-calorie foods.

Impact on Health: Obesity increases the risk of various health issues, including diabetes, joint problems, and cardiovascular diseases.

Dietary Management:

- **Caloric Restriction**: Reducing caloric intake while maintaining a balanced diet is crucial for weight loss.
- **High-Protein, Low-Fat Diets**: These diets can help maintain muscle mass while promoting fat loss.
- **Increased Fiber**: Fiber can increase satiety and help reduce overall calorie consumption.

Prevention Strategies: Regular exercise, portion control, and feeding a balanced diet tailored to the pet's energy needs are key to preventing obesity.

2. Diabetes Mellitus

Etiology: Diabetes in pets is often associated with obesity and can be classified as insulin-dependent (Type I) or non-insulin-dependent (Type II).

Impact on Health: Diabetes can lead to complications such as neuropathy, cataracts, and increased susceptibility to infections.

Dietary Management:

- **Consistent Carbohydrate Intake**: For diabetic dogs, a diet with complex carbohydrates and low glycemic index helps in managing blood glucose levels.
- **High-Protein, Low-Carbohydrate Diets**: For diabetic cats, these diets mimic their natural carnivorous diet and help in regulating glucose levels.
- **Fiber**: Moderate amounts of fiber can slow glucose absorption and improve glycemic control.

Prevention Strategies: Maintaining a healthy weight, regular exercise, and feeding a balanced diet are essential in preventing diabetes.

3. Kidney Disease

Etiology: Chronic kidney disease (CKD) can result from various factors, including age, genetics, and underlying health conditions. Diet plays a role in managing the progression of CKD.

Impact on Health: CKD can lead to electrolyte imbalances, hypertension, and anemia.

Dietary Management:

- **Reduced Phosphorus**: Lowering phosphorus intake can help slow the progression of kidney disease.
- **Moderate Protein**: While protein restriction was traditionally recommended, recent studies suggest that moderate, high-quality protein is beneficial for maintaining muscle mass without overburdening the kidneys.
- **Increased Omega-3 Fatty Acids**: These can help reduce inflammation and support kidney function.

Prevention Strategies: Regular veterinary check-ups, maintaining hydration, and feeding a balanced diet can help in the early detection and management of kidney disease.

The relationship between diet and chronic health conditions in cats and dogs is complex and multifaceted. Proper nutritional management is crucial for the prevention and management of obesity, diabetes, and kidney disease. By understanding the specific dietary needs associated with these conditions, pet owners and veterinarians can work together to develop effective feeding strategies that promote optimal health and well-being for pets. Regular veterinary check-ups and monitoring are essential to adjust dietary plans as needed and ensure the overall health of cats and dogs with chronic conditions.

****

Chapter 6

Daily Nutritional Requirements for Cats

Cats have specific dietary needs that must be met to ensure their health and well-being. Their nutritional requirements vary based on factors such as age, activity level, and health status. This section provides a comprehensive overview of the daily nutritional requirements for cats, including the amounts of essential vitamins, minerals, and other nutrients needed to maintain optimal health.

1. Protein

- **Importance**: Protein is crucial for building and repairing tissues, supporting immune function, and providing energy.
- **Daily Requirement**: Adult cats require at least 6.25 grams of protein per kilogram of body weight per day. For example, a 4 kg adult cat needs at least 25 grams of protein daily.

2. Fat

- **Importance**: Fats provide energy, support cell structure, and aid in the absorption of fat-soluble vitamins.
- **Daily Requirement**: Adult cats need at least 2.5 grams of fat per kilogram of body weight per day. A 4 kg adult cat requires at least 10 grams of fat daily.

3. Carbohydrates

- **Importance**: While not essential, carbohydrates provide a source of energy and dietary fiber.

- **Daily Requirement**: There is no minimum requirement, but moderate levels are recommended for energy and fiber.

4. Vitamins

- **Vitamin A**: Essential for vision and immune function. Adult cats require at least 333 IU per kilogram of body weight per day.
- **Vitamin D**: Important for calcium and phosphorus metabolism. Adult cats need at least 3.33 IU per kilogram of body weight per day.
- **Vitamin E**: Acts as an antioxidant and supports immune function. Adult cats require at least 0.83 IU per kilogram of body weight per day.
- **Vitamin K**: Necessary for blood clotting. The exact daily requirement is not well defined, but it is typically met through a balanced diet.
- **B-Vitamins**: Including thiamine (0.56 mg/kg/day), riboflavin (0.56 mg/kg/day), niacin (5.56 mg/kg/day), pantothenic acid (0.56 mg/kg/day), pyridoxine (0.4 mg/kg/day), biotin, folic acid (0.09 mg/kg/day), and cobalamin. These are important for energy metabolism and neurological health.

5. Minerals

- **Calcium and Phosphorus**: Essential for bone health. Adult cats require a calcium-to-phosphorus ratio of about 1:1 to 2:1. Daily calcium needs are approximately 50 mg/kg, and phosphorus needs are about 40 mg/kg.
- **Potassium**: Needed for nerve function and muscle control. Adult cats require at least 0.6 grams per kilogram of body

weight per day.

- **Sodium and Chloride**: Important for fluid balance and nerve function. Adult cats need at least 0.2 grams of sodium and 0.3 grams of chloride per kilogram of body weight per day.
- **Magnesium**: Involved in many enzymatic reactions. Adult cats require at least 0.02 grams per kilogram of body weight per day.
- **Iron**: Necessary for oxygen transport. Adult cats need at least 1 mg per kilogram of body weight per day.
- **Zinc**: Important for skin health and immune function. Adult cats require at least 2 mg per kilogram of body weight per day.
- **Copper**: Involved in iron metabolism. Adult cats need at least 0.15 mg per kilogram of body weight per day.

6. Amino Acids

- **Taurine**: Essential for heart health and vision. Adult cats require at least 10 mg per kilogram of body weight per day.
- **Arginine**: Vital for detoxifying ammonia. Adult cats need at least 1.25 grams per kilogram of body weight per day.
- **Methionine and Cysteine**: Important for skin and coat health. The combined requirement is at least 1.5 grams per kilogram of body weight per day.

7. Water

- **Importance**: Water is essential for hydration, digestion, and overall bodily functions.
- **Daily Requirement**: Cats should always have access to fresh, clean water. They typically need about 50-60 ml of water per kilogram of body weight per day.

Meeting the daily nutritional requirements of cats is essential for their health and longevity. A balanced diet that provides the right amounts of high-quality proteins, fats, vitamins, minerals, and water will support their physiological needs and promote overall well-being. It's important to consult with a veterinarian or a pet nutritionist to tailor the diet to your cat's individual needs and to adjust it as necessary throughout their life stages. Regular check-ups can help ensure that your cat's nutritional needs are being met and can help prevent or manage chronic health conditions.

****

Chapter 7

Daily Nutritional Requirements For Dogs

Dogs, like humans, require a balanced diet to maintain optimal health. Their nutritional needs vary depending on factors such as age, size, activity level, and health status. Understanding these requirements is crucial for ensuring that dogs receive all the essential nutrients they need for growth, maintenance, and overall well-being. This section provides a detailed overview of the daily nutritional needs of dogs, including vitamins, minerals, proteins, fats, and carbohydrates.

1. Proteins

Importance: Proteins are vital for building and repairing tissues, supporting immune function, and providing energy.

Daily Requirement: Adult dogs require a minimum of 18% protein on a dry matter basis in their diet. Puppies and lactating females need higher levels, around 22-25%.

Sources: High-quality animal-based proteins such as chicken, beef, lamb, and fish are excellent sources for dogs.

2. Fats

Importance: Fats provide energy, support cell structure, and aid in the absorption of fat-soluble vitamins. They also provide essential fatty acids that dogs cannot synthesize on their own.

Daily Requirement: Adult dogs need a minimum of 5% fat in their diet, but 10-15% is commonly recommended for optimal health.

Sources: Animal fats and oils like fish oil, flaxseed oil, and chicken fat are good sources of essential fatty acids, including omega-3 and omega-6.

3. Carbohydrates

Importance: While not technically essential, carbohydrates provide a source of energy and dietary fiber, which aids in digestion and promotes a healthy gut.

Daily Requirement: There is no minimum requirement, but moderate levels are recommended for energy and fiber.

Sources: Whole grains, vegetables, and fruits can provide digestible carbohydrates and fiber.

4. Vitamins

- **Vitamin A**: Essential for vision and immune function. Adult dogs require at least 3,333 IU per kilogram of body weight per day.
- **Vitamin D**: Important for calcium and phosphorus metabolism and bone health. Adult dogs need at least 333 IU per kilogram of body weight per day.
- **Vitamin E**: Acts as an antioxidant and supports immune function. Adult dogs require at least 33 IU per kilogram of body weight per day.
- **Vitamin K**: Necessary for blood clotting and bone metabolism. The exact daily requirement is not well defined, but it is typically met through a balanced diet.
- **B-Vitamins**: Including thiamine, riboflavin, niacin, pantothenic acid, pyridoxine, biotin, folic acid, and cobalamin, are important for energy metabolism and neurological health.

5. Minerals

- **Calcium and Phosphorus**: Essential for bone health. Adult dogs require a calcium-to-phosphorus ratio of about 1:1 to 2:1. Daily calcium needs are approximately 100 mg/kg, and phosphorus needs are about 75 mg/kg.
- **Potassium**: Needed for nerve function and muscle control. Adult dogs require at least 0.6 grams per kilogram of body weight per day.
- **Sodium and Chloride**: Important for fluid balance and nerve function. Adult dogs need at least 0.3 grams of sodium and 0.45 grams of chloride per kilogram of body weight per day.
- **Magnesium**: Involved in many enzymatic reactions. Adult dogs require at least 0.04 grams per kilogram of body weight per day.
- **Iron**: Necessary for oxygen transport. Adult dogs need at least 7.5 mg per kilogram of body weight per day.
- **Zinc**: Important for skin health and immune function. Adult dogs require at least 15 mg per kilogram of body weight per day.
- **Copper**: Involved in iron metabolism. Adult dogs need at least 1.5 mg per kilogram of body weight per day.

6. Water

Importance: Water is crucial for hydration, digestion, and overall bodily functions.

Daily Requirement: Dogs should always have access to fresh, clean water. They typically need about 60 ml of water per kilogram of body weight per day.

Meeting the daily nutritional requirements of dogs is essential for their health and longevity. A balanced diet that provides the right amounts of high-quality proteins, fats, vitamins, minerals, and water will support their physiological needs and promote overall well-being.

****

Chapter 8

Decoding Nutritional and Ingredient Labels on Commercial Pet Food Packaging

Understanding the Guaranteed Analysis: A Guide to Pet Food Labels

When selecting commercial pet food, it's crucial to understand the guaranteed analysis (GA) provided on the packaging. This section of the label offers vital information about the nutritional content of the food, including percentages of crude protein, fat, fiber, and moisture. By interpreting these values correctly, pet owners can make informed choices to meet their pet's dietary needs.

1. Crude Protein

- **Importance**: Protein is essential for building and repairing tissues, supporting the immune system, and providing energy. It's especially crucial for growing puppies and kittens, as well as active and pregnant or lactating pets.
- **Interpreting GA**: The percentage of crude protein indicates the minimum amount of protein present in the food. Look for a minimum of 18-26% for adult dogs and 26-30% for adult cats. Higher percentages may be necessary for specific life stages or conditions.
- **Quality Considerations**: Not all protein sources are equal. Animal-based proteins are generally more digestible and provide a complete amino acid profile. Check the ingredient list for high-quality sources like chicken, beef, fish, or eggs.

2. Crude Fat

- **Importance**: Fats are a concentrated energy source and are vital for maintaining healthy skin and coat, absorbing fat-soluble vitamins, and supporting cell function.
- **Interpreting GA**: The crude fat percentage represents the minimum amount of fat in the food. Adult dogs typically require at least 5-15% fat, while adult cats need around 9-15%. Puppies, kittens, and lactating pets may need higher levels.
- **Quality Considerations**: Look for foods with identifiable fat sources such as chicken fat, fish oil, or flaxseed oil. These provide essential fatty acids like omega-3 and omega-6, which are crucial for overall health.

3. Crude Fiber

- **Importance**: Fiber aids in digestion, helps regulate blood sugar levels, and promotes a feeling of fullness, which can be beneficial for weight management.
- **Interpreting GA**: The crude fiber percentage indicates the maximum amount of fiber in the food. Dogs generally benefit from diets with 2-4% fiber, while cats require less, typically around 1-3%.
- **Quality Considerations**: Sources of fiber include vegetables, fruits, and whole grains. Avoid foods with excessive fiber, as they can interfere with nutrient absorption and lead to digestive issues.

4. Moisture

- **Importance**: Moisture content is crucial for hydration and can impact the food's caloric density. Wet foods have higher moisture levels, which can be beneficial for pets that don't drink enough water.

- **Interpreting GA**: Moisture percentages usually range from 6-10% in dry foods and 70-85% in wet foods. When comparing nutrient levels between dry and wet foods, it's essential to calculate the dry matter basis to ensure accurate comparisons.

- **Quality Considerations**: While moisture is necessary, it's important to balance it with nutrient density. Wet foods can provide hydration but may require supplementation with dry food to meet all nutritional needs.

The guaranteed analysis on pet food labels provides a snapshot of the nutritional content, but it's just one piece of the puzzle. To ensure your pet's diet is truly balanced and meets their specific needs, consider the quality and sources of the listed nutrients. Always consult with a veterinarian or a pet nutritionist when making dietary changes, especially for pets with specific health conditions. By understanding the guaranteed analysis and choosing high-quality foods, you can support your pet's health and well-being.

Identifying Key Ingredients in Commercial Pet Food

Deciphering the ingredient list on commercial pet food packaging is essential for ensuring that your cat or dog receives a nutritious and balanced diet. High-quality ingredients contribute to the overall health and well-being of your pet. This section provides guidance on recognizing these ingredients and understanding their order on the label.

1. Understanding the Ingredient Order

- **Order by Weight**: Ingredients are listed in descending order by weight, with the heaviest ingredients listed first. This includes water content, so ingredients with higher moisture levels, like fresh meats, may appear higher on the list.
- **Splitting**: Be aware of ingredient splitting, where similar ingredients are listed separately to lower their apparent contribution. For example, corn may be listed as cornmeal, corn gluten, and corn bran to avoid having it appear as the primary ingredient.

2. High-Quality Protein Sources

- **Whole Meats**: Look for whole meats like chicken, beef, fish, or lamb listed as the first ingredient. These provide essential amino acids and are more easily digestible.
- **Meat Meals**: Meals, such as chicken meal or fish meal, are concentrated sources of protein with most of the moisture removed. They can be a valuable protein source if from a specified animal.
- **By-Products**: Be cautious of by-products, which can vary in quality. Look for named by-products (e.g., chicken by-product meal) from reputable sources.

3. Healthy Fats

- **Named Animal Fats**: Look for specific fat sources like chicken fat or salmon oil. These provide essential fatty acids and are preferable to generic "animal fat."
- **Plant Oils**: Flaxseed oil, sunflower oil, and coconut oil are good sources of omega-3 and omega-6 fatty acids, which

support skin and coat health.

4. Whole Grains and Vegetables

- **Whole Grains**: Whole grains like brown rice, barley, and oats provide carbohydrates, fiber, and essential nutrients. They are generally preferable to refined grains.
- **Vegetables**: Vegetables like carrots, peas, and sweet potatoes are excellent sources of vitamins, minerals, and fiber. Look for whole, named vegetables in the ingredient list.

5. Avoiding Unnecessary Additives

- **Artificial Colors and Flavors**: These additives have no nutritional value and are often used to make the food more appealing to pet owners rather than pets.
- **Preservatives**: Natural preservatives like tocopherols (vitamin E) or ascorbic acid (vitamin C) are preferable to artificial preservatives like BHA, BHT, or ethoxyquin.

6. Special Ingredients for Digestive Health

- **Fiber Sources**: Ingredients like beet pulp, pumpkin, or inulin provide fiber, which supports digestive health and can be beneficial for pets with sensitive stomachs.
- **Probiotics**: Some foods include added probiotics to promote a healthy gut microbiome. Look for specific strains listed on the label.

Identifying key ingredients in commercial pet food is crucial for providing your pet with a nutritious diet. High-quality proteins, healthy fats, whole grains, and vegetables are the foundation of a balanced diet. Avoiding unnecessary additives and considering special ingredients for digestive health can further support your pet's well-being.

Deciphering Additives and Preservatives in Commercial Pet Food

Additives and preservatives are commonly found in commercial pet foods to enhance flavor, appearance, and shelf life. While some of these substances are necessary and safe, others may be of concern, especially for pets with sensitive digestive systems. Understanding these additives and their purposes can help pet owners make informed choices about their pet's diet.

1. Additives

Flavor Enhancers:

- **Purpose**: To make the food more palatable for pets.
- **Common Types**: Animal digest, broth, and natural flavors.
- **Considerations**: While generally safe, some pets may have sensitivities to specific flavorings.

Coloring Agents:

- **Purpose**: To improve the visual appeal of the food.
- **Common Types**: Caramel color, titanium dioxide, and artificial colors (e.g., Red 40, Blue 2).
- **Considerations**: Artificial colors are often unnecessary and may be linked to health issues in some pets. Natural coloring from fruits and vegetables is preferable.

Texturizers and Binders:

- **Purpose**: To maintain the consistency and shape of the food.
- **Common Types**: Gums (e.g., guar gum, carrageenan), gelatin, and wheat gluten.
- **Considerations**: Some pets may have sensitivities to certain gums or gluten. Carrageenan, in particular, has been a subject of debate regarding its safety.

2. Preservatives

Natural Preservatives:

- **Purpose**: To extend shelf life by preventing spoilage from bacteria, mold, and oxidation.
- **Common Types**: Mixed tocopherols (vitamin E), ascorbic acid (vitamin C), and rosemary extract.
- **Considerations**: Natural preservatives are generally considered safe and beneficial for pets.

Artificial Preservatives:

- **Purpose**: Similar to natural preservatives, but often more effective and longer-lasting.
- **Common Types**: Butylated hydroxyanisole (BHA), butylated hydroxytoluene (BHT), and ethoxyquin.
- **Considerations**: These preservatives have been associated with potential health risks, and their use is controversial. Ethoxyquin, in particular, has been linked to liver and kidney issues in pets.

3. Antioxidants

- **Purpose**: To prevent fats and oils in the food from becoming rancid.
- **Common Types**: Vitamin E (tocopherols), vitamin C (ascorbic acid), and synthetic antioxidants.
- **Considerations**: Natural antioxidants like vitamins E and C are preferred over synthetic options for their safety and health benefits.

4. Emulsifiers and Stabilizers

- **Purpose**: To keep water and fat from separating in canned or moist foods.
- **Common Types**: Lecithin, agar-agar, and carrageenan.
- **Considerations**: While generally safe, some pets may have sensitivities to these ingredients.

5. Choosing Pet Foods with Safe Additives and Preservatives

- **Read Labels Carefully**: Look for natural preservatives as well as flavorings and avoid artificial colors and controversial additives.
- **Consult with a Veterinarian**: Especially for pets with sensitive digestive systems or food allergies, a vet can recommend suitable diets.
- **Consider Homemade or Fresh Foods**: For pets with severe sensitivities, homemade or fresh diets may offer more control over ingredients.

Additives and preservatives are common in commercial pet foods, serving various purposes from enhancing flavor to extending shelf life. However, not all these substances are created equal, and some may pose risks to pets with sensitive digestive systems. By understanding the types and purposes of these additives, pet owners can make informed decisions about their pet's diet, prioritizing natural and safe ingredients for optimal health.

Interpreting Nutritional Adequacy Statements on Pet Food Labels

Nutritional adequacy statements are crucial components of pet food labels, offering essential information about the nutritional value of the food and its suitability for different life stages and health conditions. Understanding these statements helps pet owners ensure their pets receive a balanced diet that meets their specific needs.

1. Significance of Nutritional Adequacy Statements

- **Purpose**: These statements indicate whether the pet food provides complete and balanced nutrition for a specific life stage or health condition.
- **Regulation**: In many countries, pet food labeling is regulated by authorities such as the Association of American Feed Control Officials (AAFCO) in the United States, which sets guidelines for nutritional adequacy.

2. Common Nutritional Adequacy Statements

- **"Complete and Balanced"**: This statement means the food provides all necessary nutrients in the correct proportions for maintaining overall health. It should be accompanied by a life stage or condition specification, such as "for adult maintenance" or "for growth."
- **"For All Life Stages"**: Indicates the food meets nutritional

requirements for both growth and adult maintenance, making it suitable for pets of any age.

- **"For Growth"**: Formulated for puppies or kittens, these foods provide higher levels of protein, fat, and other nutrients needed for proper development.
- **"For Adult Maintenance"**: Designed for adult pets, these foods offer balanced nutrition for maintaining health but may not be suitable for growing, pregnant, or lactating animals.
- **"For Senior/Mature"**: Tailored for older pets, these foods may have lower calorie content and adjusted nutrient levels to meet the needs of aging animals.

3. Ensuring the Food Meets Specific Requirements

- **Life Stage Considerations**: Choose food that matches your pet's current life stage, as their nutritional needs change with age.
- **Health Conditions**: For pets with specific health issues, such as kidney disease or obesity, select a diet formulated to address those conditions, often labeled as "veterinary" or "prescription" diets.
- **Activity Level**: Active pets may require higher calorie diets, while less active pets may need lower calorie options to prevent weight gain.

4. Reading Beyond the Statement

- **Ingredient Quality**: Check the ingredient list for high-quality sources of protein, fats, and carbohydrates. Whole meats, named animal fats, and whole grains are indicators of a better-quality food.

- **Nutrient Ratios**: Ensure the food provides appropriate ratios of protein, fat, and carbohydrates for your pet's needs. For example, cats require higher protein and lower carbohydrate levels than dogs.
- **Additional Nutrients**: Look for the inclusion of essential vitamins, minerals, and fatty acids. Omega-3 fatty acids, for example, support skin and coat health, while antioxidants like vitamins E and C support immune health.

5. Special Diets and Claims

- **Grain-Free and Limited Ingredient Diets**: These diets may be beneficial for pets with allergies or sensitivities. However, it's important to ensure they still meet all nutritional requirements.
- **Organic and Natural Claims**: Understand that these terms have specific definitions in pet food labeling and may not always equate to better nutritional value.

6. Consulting with a Professional

- **Veterinarian Guidance**: Always consult with a veterinarian or a pet nutritionist when selecting a diet, especially for pets with health conditions or special dietary needs. They can provide personalized recommendations based on your pet's specific requirements.

Nutritional adequacy statements on pet food labels are essential tools for ensuring that your pet receives a diet that meets their nutritional needs. By understanding these statements and considering factors such as life stage, health conditions, and ingredient quality, pet owners can make informed choices that support their pet's health and well-being.

Navigating Special Dietary Claims:

Choosing the Right Food for Your Pet's Digestive Health

The pet food market is flooded with products boasting various dietary claims, such as "grain-free," "limited ingredient," and "sensitive stomach" formulas. While these claims can guide pet owners in selecting a suitable diet for their pets with digestive issues, it's essential to understand what these terms mean and how they relate to your pet's specific needs.

1. Grain-Free Diets

Claim Overview: Grain-free pet foods are formulated without grains like wheat, corn, or rice, which are often used as carbohydrate sources in traditional pet foods.

Benefits:

- **Allergy Management**: Some pets may have allergies or sensitivities to specific grains, leading to digestive issues. Grain-free diets can be beneficial in these cases.
- **Alternative Carbohydrates**: These diets often use alternative carbohydrate sources such as sweet potatoes or peas, which may be more digestible for some pets.

Considerations:

- **Nutritional Balance**: Ensure the grain-free diet provides complete and balanced nutrition for your pet's life stage and health status.
- **Recent Concerns**: There have been concerns about potential links between grain-free diets and heart disease in dogs (dilated cardiomyopathy). Consult with a veterinarian before

switching to a grain-free diet.

2. Limited Ingredient Diets (LID)

Claim Overview: Limited ingredient diets are formulated with a smaller number of ingredients to minimize the risk of food sensitivities or allergies.

Benefits:

- **Simplified Ingredients**: Fewer ingredients mean fewer potential allergens, making it easier to identify and avoid problematic foods.
- **Digestive Support**: LIDs can be beneficial for pets with sensitive stomachs or inflammatory bowel disease by reducing dietary irritants.

Considerations:

- **Nutritional Adequacy**: Ensure the limited ingredient diet provides all the necessary nutrients for your pet's health.
- **Protein Sources**: Look for a high-quality, novel protein source (e.g., duck, venison) that your pet has not been exposed to before.

3. Sensitive Stomach Formulas

Claim Overview: These formulas are designed for pets with digestive issues, offering easily digestible ingredients and added digestive support.

Benefits:

- **Gentle Ingredients**: Formulated with highly digestible

proteins, carbohydrates, and fats to ease digestion.

- **Added Supplements**: Often enriched with prebiotics, probiotics, or digestive enzymes to support gut health.

Considerations:

- **Individual Needs**: What works for one pet may not work for another. Monitor your pet's response to the diet and adjust as needed.
- **Veterinary Guidance**: Consult with a veterinarian to ensure the sensitive stomach formula addresses your pet's specific digestive concerns.

4. Choosing the Right Diet

- **Consult a Veterinarian**: Always seek professional advice when selecting a diet for a pet with digestive issues. A veterinarian can help determine the underlying cause and recommend an appropriate diet.
- **Read Labels Carefully**: Understand the ingredients and nutritional information to ensure the diet meets your pet's needs.
- **Transition Slowly**: When switching to a new diet, gradually introduce the new food over several days to prevent digestive upset.

Special dietary claims like "grain-free," "limited ingredient," and "sensitive stomach" can provide valuable guidance for pet owners seeking to improve their pets' digestive health. However, it's crucial to understand the meaning behind these claims, ensure the diet is nutritionally balanced, and consult with a veterinarian to address your pet's specific needs. By doing so, you can choose the right food to support your pet's digestive well-being and overall health.

****

Chapter 9

Unveiling Hidden Ingredients In Commercial Pet Foods

Deciphering Ingredient Lists in Cat and Dog Foods

Understanding the ingredients in commercial cat and dog foods is crucial for pet owners, especially those with pets suffering from digestive issues. Ingredient lists can often be complex, with some components disguised under technical or generic terms.

1. The Basics of Ingredient Lists

- **Order of Listing**: Ingredients are listed in descending order by weight. This means the first few ingredients are present in the highest quantities.
- **Naming Conventions**: Ingredients must be named according to regulatory guidelines, which can vary by country. For example, the Association of American Feed Control Officials (AAFCO) sets standards in the United States.

2. Protein Sources

- **Whole Meats**: Terms like "chicken" or "beef" refer to the muscle tissue of the animal, which is a high-quality protein source.
- **Meat Meals**: Ingredients like "chicken meal" or "fish meal" indicate that the meat has been rendered (cooked down) to remove moisture and fat, concentrating the protein.
- **By-Products**: Terms like "chicken by-product meal" refer to parts of the animal other than muscle meat, such as organs.

While not necessarily lower in quality, they can vary in digestibility.

3. Fat Sources

- **Named Animal Fats**: Ingredients like "chicken fat" or "salmon oil" are considered high-quality fat sources, providing essential fatty acids.
- **Generic Fats**: Terms like "animal fat" or "poultry fat" are less specific and can indicate a mix of fats from various sources, which might be of lower quality.

4. Carbohydrate Sources

- **Whole Grains**: Ingredients like "brown rice" or "barley" are whole grains that provide carbohydrates, fiber, and nutrients.
- **Grain Fractions**: Terms like "rice bran" or "corn gluten meal" indicate parts of the grain, which can be used as filler or protein sources but may be less digestible.
- **Vegetables and Legumes**: Ingredients like "peas" or "sweet potatoes" are carbohydrate sources that also provide fiber and nutrients.

5. Fiber Sources

- **Fiber Additives**: Ingredients like "beet pulp" or "cellulose" are added to pet foods as fiber sources, which can aid in digestion.
- **Natural Fiber Sources**: Whole vegetables and grains also contribute to the fiber content of the food.

6. Vitamins and Minerals

- **Supplements**: Ingredients like "vitamin E supplement" or "zinc sulfate" are added to ensure the food meets the nutritional needs of pets.
- **Chelated Minerals**: Terms like "zinc amino acid chelate" indicate minerals bound to amino acids for better absorption.

7. Additives and Preservatives

- **Preservatives**: Ingredients like "mixed tocopherols" (a form of vitamin E) are natural preservatives, while "BHA" and "BHT" are synthetic preservatives with potential health concerns.
- **Flavorings and Colorings**: Terms like "natural flavor" or "artificial colors" are added to enhance the palatability and appearance of the food but offer no nutritional value.

8. Understanding "Natural" and "Organic" Claims

- **Natural**: This term is regulated and means the product does not contain artificial flavors, colors, or preservatives. However, it does not indicate the quality of the ingredients.
- **Organic**: Organic pet foods must meet strict production and processing standards, such as using ingredients grown without synthetic pesticides or fertilizers.

9. Deciphering Marketing Terms

- **Holistic**: This term is not legally defined or regulated in pet food labeling and can be used freely by manufacturers without any specific standards.
- **Human-Grade**: This term implies that the ingredients are suitable for human consumption, but it's not officially

regulated in most regions.

Deciphering ingredient lists in cat and dog foods can be challenging, but understanding the meaning behind common terms can help pet owners make informed choices. Look for high-quality protein sources, named fats, whole grains, and natural preservatives. Be wary of generic terms, fillers, and artificial additives, especially if your pet has digestive sensitivities.

Common Hidden Ingredients in Commercial Cat and Dog Food and Their Impact

Commercial cat and dog foods often contain ingredients that are not immediately recognizable to the average pet owner. Understanding these hidden ingredients, such as by-products, fillers, and artificial additives, is essential for making informed decisions about your pet's diet. This section explores these ingredients and their potential impacts on pet health.

1. By-Products

- **Definition**: By-products are the parts of animals that are not typically consumed by humans, including organs, bones, and other tissues.
- **Impact**: While some by-products can be nutritious sources of protein and other nutrients, their quality can vary widely. Low-quality by-products may contain indigestible or less nutritious parts, which can contribute to digestive issues in pets.

2. Fillers

- **Definition**: Fillers are ingredients used to add bulk to pet food without providing significant nutritional value. Common fillers include corn, wheat, soy, and cellulose.
- **Impact**: Fillers can lead to weight gain and may cause digestive problems in pets with sensitivities or allergies to these ingredients. They may also result in less nutrient-dense food, requiring pets to eat more to meet their nutritional needs.

3. Artificial Preservatives

- **Definition**: Artificial preservatives, such as BHA, BHT, and ethoxyquin, are used to extend the shelf life of pet food.
- **Impact**: Some artificial preservatives have been linked to health concerns, including potential carcinogenic effects and allergic reactions. Pets with sensitive digestive systems may also experience gastrointestinal upset from these additives.

4. Artificial Colors and Flavors

- **Definition**: These additives are used to enhance the appearance and taste of pet food to make it more appealing to pets and their owners.
- **Impact**: Artificial colors and flavors offer no nutritional value and may trigger allergic reactions or sensitivities in some pets. They are often associated with low-quality pet foods.

5. Meat and Bone Meal

- **Definition**: Meat and bone meal is a rendered product from animal tissues, including bones and offal.
- **Impact**: The nutritional value of meat and bone meal can

vary significantly depending on the source. In some cases, it may contain high levels of minerals like phosphorus and calcium, which can be problematic for pets with kidney disease or other health issues.

6. Grains and Gluten

- **Definition**: Grains such as corn, wheat, and barley, as well as gluten, are often used as sources of carbohydrates and protein in pet food.
- **Impact**: While grains can be a healthy part of a pet's diet, some pets may have allergies or intolerances to specific grains or gluten, leading to digestive problems and skin issues.

7. Sweeteners

- **Definition**: Sweeteners like corn syrup, sugar, and molasses are sometimes added to pet foods to enhance palatability.
- **Impact**: Added sweeteners can contribute to obesity, dental problems, and blood sugar imbalances in pets. They are generally considered unnecessary in a well-balanced diet.

8. Chemical Flavor Enhancers

- **Definition**: Flavor enhancers, such as monosodium glutamate (MSG), are added to make pet food more palatable.
- **Impact**: These chemicals can cause adverse reactions in some pets, including allergic reactions and digestive issues.

9. Soy and Soy Products

- **Definition**: Soy is used as a source of protein and as a filler in some pet foods.

- **Impact**: Soy can be difficult for some pets to digest and may cause gastrointestinal upset. It can also be a common allergen for pets.

10. Rendered Fat

- **Definition**: Rendered fat is added to pet food for flavor and energy.
- **Impact**: While fat is an essential nutrient, rendered fat from unspecified sources can be of variable quality and may increase the risk of bacterial contamination or rancidity.

Understanding the hidden ingredients in commercial cat and dog food is crucial for pet owners, especially those with pets suffering from digestive issues. By being aware of the potential impacts of by-products, fillers, artificial additives, and other frequently used ingredients, pet owners can make more informed choices about their pet's diet.

Identifying Allergens and Irritants in Pet Foods

Allergies and sensitivities to certain ingredients in pet foods can lead to a variety of health issues, including digestive problems, skin irritations, and other allergic reactions. Identifying potential allergens and irritants is crucial for pet owners, especially for those with pets suffering from digestive issues.

1. Common Allergens in Pet Foods

- **Proteins**: Animal proteins like beef, chicken, dairy, and eggs are among the most common allergens for pets. Some pets may also react to certain fish or lamb proteins.
- **Grains**: Grains such as wheat, corn, and soy are common

allergens that can trigger digestive issues and skin reactions in sensitive pets.

- **Gluten**: Gluten, a protein found in wheat and other grains, can cause allergic reactions in pets with gluten sensitivity or celiac disease.

2. Identifying Protein Allergens

- **Single-Source Protein Diets**: To identify protein allergens, consider feeding your pet a diet with a single source of animal protein that they have not been exposed to before.
- **Hydrolyzed Protein Diets**: Hydrolyzed proteins are broken down into smaller peptides, making them less likely to trigger an allergic response. These diets can be useful for pets with severe protein allergies.

3. Grain Allergies and Alternatives

- **Grain-Free Diets**: For pets with grain allergies, grain-free diets that use alternative carbohydrate sources like potatoes, peas, or lentils can be beneficial.
- **Whole Grains**: If your pet is not allergic to all grains, consider choosing diets with whole grains like brown rice or barley, which are less likely to cause sensitivities than processed grains.

4. Artificial Additives and Preservatives

- **Artificial Colors and Flavors**: These additives can sometimes trigger allergic reactions in pets. Look for foods that use natural flavors and avoid artificial colors.
- **Preservatives**: Some artificial preservatives, like BHA, BHT,

and ethoxyquin, may cause allergic reactions. Opt for foods preserved with natural substances like vitamin E (tocopherols) or vitamin C (ascorbic acid).

5. Other Potential Irritants

- **Dairy Products**: Lactose intolerance is common in adult pets, leading to digestive issues. Avoid dairy-based ingredients if your pet shows signs of intolerance.
- **Fats and Oils**: While essential for health, some pets may be sensitive to certain fats or oils. Monitor your pet's reaction to different fat sources in their diet.

6. Conducting an Elimination Diet

- **Elimination Process**: To identify specific allergens, gradually eliminate suspect ingredients from your pet's diet and monitor for improvements in symptoms.
- **Reintroduction Phase**: After symptoms resolve, reintroduce ingredients one at a time to pinpoint the exact allergen.

7. Reading Ingredient Labels

- **Detailed Inspection**: Carefully read the ingredient list on pet food labels to identify potential allergens and irritants. Be mindful of generic terms like "animal fat" or "meat meal," which can hide specific allergens.
- **Consult a Veterinarian**: Work with a veterinarian or a pet nutritionist to develop an appropriate diet plan for your pet, especially if they have known allergies or sensitivities.

Identifying allergens and irritants in pet foods is essential for managing and preventing allergic reactions and digestive issues in pets. By understanding common allergens, choosing appropriate diets, and conducting elimination trials, pet owners can help ensure their pets enjoy a healthy and comfortable life. Always consult with a veterinary professional when addressing your pet's dietary needs, particularly if they have a history of allergies or sensitivities.

****

Chapter 10

Making the Switch to Homemade Diets

For Your Cat or Dog

The Health Benefits of Homemade Diets for Cats and Dogs

Homemade diets for cats and dogs have gained popularity among pet owners seeking to provide their furry companions with nutritious, wholesome meals. These diets offer several advantages, including improved ingredient quality, tailored nutrition, and the avoidance of artificial additives and preservatives.

1. Improved Ingredient Quality

- **Freshness**: Homemade diets allow pet owners to use fresh ingredients, ensuring that pets receive the maximum nutritional value from their meals.
- **Control Over Sources**: By preparing meals at home, owners can select high-quality, human-grade ingredients and avoid the uncertainties associated with commercial pet food production.
- **Whole Foods**: Homemade diets often incorporate whole foods, providing pets with a variety of nutrients in their natural form.

2. Tailored Nutrition

- **Individual Needs**: Homemade diets can be customized to

meet the specific nutritional requirements of each pet, taking into account factors such as age, weight, activity level, and health conditions.

- **Dietary Restrictions**: For pets with food sensitivities, allergies, or specific medical conditions, homemade diets allow for the exclusion of problematic ingredients and the inclusion of beneficial ones.
- **Balanced Meals**: With proper guidance from a veterinarian or pet nutritionist, homemade diets can be formulated to ensure a balanced intake of proteins, fats, carbohydrates, vitamins, and minerals.

3. Avoidance of Artificial Additives and Preservatives

- **Natural Ingredients**: Homemade diets typically avoid the use of artificial colors, flavors, and preservatives, reducing the risk of adverse reactions or long-term health issues.
- **Transparency**: Pet owners have complete control over what goes into their pet's food, providing peace of mind about the absence of hidden additives.

4. Enhanced Digestibility

- **Gentle on the Stomach**: Fresh, natural ingredients are often more digestible than processed commercial foods, which can be beneficial for pets with sensitive stomachs or digestive disorders.
- **Customizable Fiber Content**: Homemade diets allow for the adjustment of fiber levels to suit individual digestive needs, promoting healthy bowel movements and gut health.

5. Positive Behavioral and Physical Effects

- **Increased Enjoyment**: Many pets show a preference for the taste and variety of homemade meals over commercial foods.
- **Improved Health Markers**: Pet owners often report improvements in their pet's coat condition, energy levels, and overall vitality when switching to a homemade diet.

6. Strengthened Bond Between Pet and Owner

- **Personal Involvement**: Preparing meals for your pet can deepen the bond between you, as it involves time, effort, and care.
- **Mindful Feeding**: The process of creating homemade meals encourages pet owners to become more attuned to their pet's nutritional needs and preferences.

Challenges and Considerations

While homemade diets offer numerous benefits, they also present challenges, such as ensuring nutritional completeness, managing preparation time, and maintaining consistency. It is essential to consult with a veterinarian or a certified pet nutritionist to develop a balanced and appropriate meal plan for your pet.

Homemade diets can provide significant health benefits for cats and dogs, particularly those with digestive issues. By offering improved ingredient quality, tailored nutrition, and the avoidance of artificial additives, homemade meals can contribute to the overall well-being and longevity of pets. However, careful planning and professional guidance are crucial to ensure that these diets meet all the nutritional requirements of your furry companion.

Challenges of Transitioning to Homemade Meals for Pets

Switching to a homemade diet for cats and dogs can offer numerous health benefits, particularly for pets with digestive issues. However, this transition is not without its challenges. Pet owners need to be aware of the potential hurdles they may face, including ensuring balanced nutrition, managing preparation time, and addressing any initial digestive adjustments.

1. Ensuring Balanced Nutrition

- **Complex Nutritional Needs**: Cats and dogs have specific nutritional requirements that must be met for optimal health. Homemade diets must be carefully formulated to provide the right balance of proteins, fats, carbohydrates, vitamins, and minerals.
- **Risk of Nutrient Deficiencies**: Without proper planning, homemade diets can lead to nutrient deficiencies or imbalances, which can have serious health consequences. Common deficiencies include calcium, phosphorus, and essential vitamins.
- **Consulting Professionals**: It's crucial to work with a veterinarian or a certified pet nutritionist to develop a nutritionally complete and balanced meal plan for your pet.

2. Managing Preparation Time

- **Time-Consuming Process**: Preparing homemade meals for pets can be time-consuming, especially for owners with busy schedules. Planning, shopping for ingredients, cooking, and portioning meals require a significant time commitment.
- **Batch Cooking and Storage**: To save time, pet owners can prepare meals in bulk and store them in the refrigerator or freezer. Proper storage is essential to maintain the freshness

and nutritional value of the food.

3. Addressing Initial Digestive Adjustments

- **Transition Period**: Pets may experience digestive upset when transitioning from commercial to homemade diets. Gradual introduction of the new diet over several days to weeks can help minimize these issues.
- **Monitoring Responses**: Pet owners should closely monitor their pets for signs of digestive discomfort, such as diarrhea, vomiting, or constipation, and adjust the diet as needed.

4. Cost Considerations

- **Expense of High-Quality Ingredients**: Homemade diets often require high-quality, fresh ingredients, which can be more expensive than commercial pet food.
- **Budgeting for Supplements**: Additional supplements may be necessary to ensure nutritional completeness, adding to the overall cost of the diet.

5. Maintaining Consistency

- **Recipe Variability**: Consistency is key to providing balanced nutrition. Frequent changes in recipes or ingredient substitutions can lead to nutritional imbalances.
- **Portion Control**: Proper portion sizes are essential to prevent overfeeding or underfeeding. Pet owners need to accurately measure and adjust portions based on their pet's size, age, and activity level.

6. Handling and Safety

- **Food Safety Practices**: Safe food handling practices are crucial to prevent bacterial contamination and spoilage. This includes washing hands, using clean utensils, and cooking meats to appropriate temperatures.
- **Storing Prepared Meals**: Cooked meals should be stored in airtight containers and refrigerated or frozen promptly to maintain freshness and prevent spoilage.

7. Ongoing Monitoring and Adjustment

- **Regular Veterinary Check-ups**: Regular check-ups with a veterinarian are essential to monitor your pet's health and make any necessary adjustments to the diet.
- **Being Adaptable**: Pet owners should be prepared to make changes to the diet based on their pet's health status, preferences, and any emerging nutritional needs.

Transitioning to homemade meals for cats and dogs can be challenging, but with careful planning and attention to detail, it is possible to provide a nutritious and balanced diet that supports your pet's health and well-being. By being aware of the potential difficulties and taking proactive steps to address them, pet owners can successfully navigate the switch to homemade diets and enjoy the many benefits they offer for their pets with digestive issues.

Addressing Nutritional Concerns in

Homemade Diets for Cats and Dogs

While homemade diets offer numerous benefits for cats and dogs, especially those with digestive issues, they also present several nutritional challenges. Ensuring that homemade meals meet all essential nutrient requirements and maintaining proper portion control are critical for your pet's health.

1. Meeting Essential Nutrient Requirements

- **Understanding Nutritional Needs**: Cats and dogs have specific nutritional requirements that must be met for optimal health. These include the right balance of proteins, fats, carbohydrates, vitamins, minerals, and water.
- **Protein Quality and Quantity**: High-quality animal proteins should form the basis of the diet, providing essential amino acids like taurine for cats and arginine for dogs.
- **Fats and Fatty Acids**: Healthy fats are necessary for energy and the absorption of fat-soluble vitamins. Ensure the inclusion of omega-3 and omega-6 fatty acids for skin and coat health.
- **Vitamins and Minerals**: A homemade diet must supply all necessary vitamins and minerals in the correct amounts. Supplementation may be required to prevent deficiencies, particularly for calcium, phosphorus, and certain vitamins.

2. Formulating Balanced Meals

- **Consulting Professionals**: Work with a veterinarian or a certified pet nutritionist to develop balanced meal plans tailored to your pet's specific needs.
- **Using Nutrient Calculators**: Online tools and resources can help calculate the nutritional content of homemade meals to ensure they meet your pet's requirements.
- **Diverse Ingredients**: Incorporate a variety of ingredients to provide a broad spectrum of nutrients. Rotate protein sources and include different vegetables, fruits, and grains (if

tolerated).

3. Portion Control and Feeding Guidelines

- **Determining Caloric Needs**: Calculate your pet's daily caloric requirements based on their weight, age, activity level, and any health conditions.
- **Measuring Portions**: Accurately measure meal portions to prevent overfeeding or underfeeding. Use kitchen scales or measuring cups for consistency.
- **Adjusting Portions**: Monitor your pet's weight and body condition, and adjust portion sizes as needed to maintain a healthy weight.

4. Supplementing Homemade Diets

- **Identifying Gaps**: Analyze the nutritional content of your homemade meals to identify any potential gaps or deficiencies.
- **Choosing Supplements**: Select high-quality supplements to address specific needs, such as calcium for bone health or fish oil for omega-3 fatty acids.
- **Integrating Supplements**: Incorporate supplements into your pet's meals according to the recommended dosages, ensuring they are well-mixed and palatable.

5. Monitoring and Adjusting the Diet

- **Regular Veterinary Check-ups**: Schedule regular check-ups with your veterinarian to monitor your pet's health and nutritional status.
- **Observing Health Changes**: Watch for any signs of

nutritional deficiencies or excesses, such as changes in coat condition, energy levels, or digestive function.

- **Adjusting the Diet**: Be prepared to make adjustments to the diet based on your pet's evolving needs, health status, and preferences.

6. Special Considerations for Pets with Digestive Issues

- **Easily Digestible Ingredients**: Choose ingredients that are gentle on the digestive system, such as lean proteins and well-cooked grains or vegetables.
- **Managing Food Sensitivities**: Avoid known allergens or irritants and consider an elimination diet to identify trigger foods.
- **Probiotics and Prebiotics**: Incorporate probiotics and prebiotics to support gut health and aid digestion.

Addressing nutritional concerns in homemade diets for cats and dogs requires careful planning, knowledge of your pet's needs, and ongoing monitoring. By ensuring balanced nutrition and proper portion control, you can provide your pet with a diet that supports their overall health and well-being.

****

Chapter 11

Recipes For Homemade Cat Food

Homemade Cat Food Recipes for Normal Digestion

1. Chicken and Rice Delight

- 2 cups cooked, shredded chicken
- 1 cup cooked brown rice
- 1 tablespoon cooked, mashed carrot
- 1/4 teaspoon salmon oil

2. Turkey and Vegetable Medley

- 2 cups cooked, ground turkey
- 1/2 cup steamed broccoli, mashed
- 1/2 cup steamed carrots, mashed
- 1/4 teaspoon fish oil

3. Beef and Pumpkin Puree

- 2 cups cooked, ground beef (lean)
- 1 cup pureed pumpkin (canned, unsweetened)
- 1/4 teaspoon flaxseed oil

4. Tuna and Sweet Potato Feast

- 2 cups cooked, flaked tuna (in water)
- 1 cup cooked, mashed sweet potato
- 1/4 teaspoon olive oil

5. Salmon and Pea Pâté

- 2 cups cooked, flaked salmon
- 1/2 cup cooked peas, mashed
- 1/4 teaspoon coconut oil

6. Chicken Liver and Brown Rice Blend

- 1 cup cooked, chopped chicken liver
- 1 cup cooked brown rice
- 1/2 cup steamed spinach, chopped
- 1/4 teaspoon fish oil

7. Rabbit and Zucchini Mix

- 2 cups cooked, ground rabbit
- 1/2 cup steamed zucchini, mashed
- 1/4 teaspoon sunflower oil

8. Duck and Green Bean Combo

- 2 cups cooked, shredded duck
- 1/2 cup steamed green beans, mashed
- 1/4 teaspoon hemp oil

9. Turkey and Cranberry Sauce

- 2 cups cooked, ground turkey
- 1/4 cup unsweetened cranberry sauce
- 1/2 cup cooked quinoa
- 1/4 teaspoon salmon oil

10. Chicken and Egg Breakfast

- 1 cup cooked, shredded chicken
- 1 hard-boiled egg, chopped

- 1/2 cup cooked oatmeal
- 1/4 teaspoon olive oil

11. Sardine and Spinach Surprise

- 1 cup cooked, mashed sardines (in water)
- 1/2 cup steamed spinach, chopped
- 1/2 cup cooked barley
- 1/4 teaspoon coconut oil

12. Lamb and Mint Stew

- 2 cups cooked, ground lamb
- 1/4 cup fresh mint leaves, chopped
- 1 cup cooked, mashed butternut squash
- 1/4 teaspoon flaxseed oil

13. Venison and Blueberry Bliss

- 2 cups cooked, ground venison
- 1/4 cup fresh blueberries
- 1/2 cup cooked millet
- 1/4 teaspoon sunflower oil

14. Quail and Parsley Pâté

- 2 cups cooked, chopped quail meat
- 1/4 cup fresh parsley, chopped
- 1/2 cup cooked, mashed parsnips
- 1/4 teaspoon hemp oil

15. Mackerel and Carrot Cake

- 2 cups cooked, flaked mackerel

- 1/2 cup steamed carrots, mashed
- 1/2 cup cooked brown rice
- 1/4 teaspoon olive oil

Preparation Tips:

- Always remove bones from meat and fish.
- Cook all meats thoroughly to kill any harmful bacteria.
- Steam or boil vegetables until soft, then mash or puree for easy digestion.
- Cool the meals before serving to your cat.
- Store leftovers in the refrigerator for up to 3 days or freeze for longer storage.

Homemade Cat Food Recipes for Cats with Digestive Diseases or Illnesses

1. Gentle Chicken and Rice

- 2 cups boiled, shredded chicken breast
- 1 cup cooked white rice
- 1/4 teaspoon fish oil
- 1/4 teaspoon taurine supplement

2. Soothing Turkey and Pumpkin Puree

- 2 cups boiled, ground turkey
- 1/2 cup pureed pumpkin (unsweetened)
- 1/4 teaspoon coconut oil
- 1/4 teaspoon taurine supplement

3. Digestible Fish and Sweet Potato

- 2 cups boiled, flaked white fish (e.g., cod)
- 1 cup cooked, mashed sweet potato
- 1/4 teaspoon olive oil
- 1/4 teaspoon taurine supplement

4. Low-Fat Beef and Carrot Stew

- 2 cups boiled, lean ground beef
- 1/2 cup steamed, mashed carrots
- 1/4 teaspoon flaxseed oil
- 1/4 teaspoon taurine supplement

5. Hypoallergenic Rabbit and Pea

- 2 cups boiled, ground rabbit
- 1/2 cup cooked peas, mashed
- 1/4 teaspoon sunflower oil
- 1/4 teaspoon taurine supplement

6. Easy-to-Digest Lamb and Zucchini

- 2 cups boiled, ground lamb
- 1/2 cup steamed, mashed zucchini
- 1/4 teaspoon hemp oil
- 1/4 teaspoon taurine supplement

7. Sensitive Stomach Chicken Liver Pâté

- 1 cup boiled, chopped chicken liver
- 1 cup cooked white rice
- 1/4 teaspoon salmon oil
- 1/4 teaspoon taurine supplement

8. Venison and Green Bean Blend

- 2 cups boiled, ground venison
- 1/2 cup steamed, mashed green beans
- 1/4 teaspoon coconut oil
- 1/4 teaspoon taurine supplement

9. Quail and Butternut Squash

- 2 cups boiled, chopped quail meat
- 1/2 cup cooked, mashed butternut squash
- 1/4 teaspoon olive oil
- 1/4 teaspoon taurine supplement

10. Low-Fat Turkey and Oatmeal

- 2 cups boiled, ground turkey breast
- 1/2 cup cooked oatmeal
- 1/4 teaspoon flaxseed oil
- 1/4 teaspoon taurine supplement

11. Duck and Parsnip Puree

- 2 cups boiled, shredded duck meat
- 1/2 cup steamed, mashed parsnips
- 1/4 teaspoon sunflower oil
- 1/4 teaspoon taurine supplement

12. Pheasant and Cauliflower Mash

- 2 cups boiled, chopped pheasant meat
- 1/2 cup steamed, mashed cauliflower
- 1/4 teaspoon hemp oil

- 1/4 teaspoon taurine supplement

13. Whitefish and Broccoli Rice

- 2 cups boiled, flaked whitefish
- 1/2 cup cooked, finely chopped broccoli
- 1/4 teaspoon olive oil
- 1/4 teaspoon taurine supplement

14. Lean Bison and Spinach

- 2 cups boiled, ground bison
- 1/2 cup steamed, chopped spinach
- 1/4 teaspoon coconut oil
- 1/4 teaspoon taurine supplement

15. Chicken and Rice Soup

- 2 cups boiled, shredded chicken breast
- 1 cup cooked white rice
- 1 cup low-sodium chicken broth (no onions or garlic)
- 1/4 teaspoon fish oil
- 1/4 teaspoon taurine supplement

16. Fish and Rice Porridge

- 2 cups boiled, flaked white fish (e.g., tilapia)
- 1 cup cooked white rice
- 1 cup low-sodium fish broth
- 1/4 teaspoon olive oil
- 1/4 teaspoon taurine supplement

17. Turkey and Rice Meatballs

- 2 cups boiled, ground turkey
- 1 cup cooked white rice
- 1/4 teaspoon coconut oil
- 1/4 teaspoon taurine supplement
- Form into small meatballs and serve

18. Boiled Chicken and Rice Patties

- 2 cups boiled, shredded chicken breast
- 1 cup cooked white rice
- 1/4 teaspoon flaxseed oil
- 1/4 teaspoon taurine supplement
- Form into small patties and serve

Preparation Tips:

- Always remove bones and skin from meats.
- Cook all ingredients thoroughly to ensure easy digestion.
- Puree or mash vegetables for better digestibility.
- Consult with a veterinarian to ensure these recipes are suitable for your cat's specific digestive condition.
- Add supplements as recommended by your vet to ensure nutritional completeness.

****

Chapter 12

Recipes For Homemade Dog Food

Homemade Dog Food Recipes for

Dogs with Normal Digestion

1. Chicken and Vegetable Medley

- 2 cups cooked, diced chicken breast
- 1 cup cooked brown rice
- 1/2 cup steamed carrots, diced
- 1/2 cup steamed green beans, chopped
- 1 tablespoon olive oil

2. Beef and Sweet Potato Stew

- 2 cups cooked, ground beef (lean)
- 1 cup cooked, mashed sweet potato
- 1/2 cup steamed peas
- 1 tablespoon flaxseed oil

3. Turkey and Rice Casserole

- 2 cups cooked, ground turkey
- 1 cup cooked brown rice
- 1/2 cup steamed broccoli, chopped
- 1/2 cup steamed zucchini, diced
- 1 tablespoon coconut oil

4. Salmon and Quinoa Dinner

- 2 cups cooked, flaked salmon
- 1 cup cooked quinoa
- 1/2 cup steamed spinach, chopped
- 1/2 cup steamed carrots, diced
- 1 tablespoon fish oil

5. Pork and Potato Delight

- 2 cups cooked, ground pork (lean)
- 1 cup cooked, cubed potatoes
- 1/2 cup steamed green beans, chopped
- 1/2 cup steamed apples, diced
- 1 tablespoon olive oil

6. Lamb and Barley Bowl

- 2 cups cooked, ground lamb
- 1 cup cooked barley
- 1/2 cup steamed peas
- 1/2 cup steamed carrots, diced
- 1 tablespoon flaxseed oil

7. Venison and Rice Pilaf

- 2 cups cooked, ground venison
- 1 cup cooked brown rice
- 1/2 cup steamed green peas
- 1/2 cup steamed sweet potatoes, diced
- 1 tablespoon coconut oil

8. Duck and Pumpkin Pie

- 2 cups cooked, shredded duck
- 1 cup cooked, mashed pumpkin
- 1/2 cup steamed peas
- 1/2 cup cooked oatmeal
- 1 tablespoon fish oil

9. Bison and Vegetable Mix

- 2 cups cooked, ground bison
- 1 cup cooked quinoa
- 1/2 cup steamed zucchini, diced
- 1/2 cup steamed carrots, diced
- 1 tablespoon olive oil

10. Chicken Liver and Rice Gourmet

- 1 cup cooked, chopped chicken liver
- 1 cup cooked brown rice
- 1/2 cup steamed green beans, chopped
- 1/2 cup steamed carrots, diced
- 1 tablespoon flaxseed oil

11. Fish and Potato Chowder

- 2 cups cooked, flaked whitefish (e.g., cod)
- 1 cup cooked, cubed potatoes
- 1/2 cup steamed peas
- 1/2 cup steamed carrots, diced
- 1 tablespoon coconut oil

12. Turkey and Barley Soup

- 2 cups cooked, ground turkey

- 1 cup cooked barley
- 1/2 cup steamed green beans, chopped
- 1/2 cup steamed carrots, diced
- 1 tablespoon fish oil

13. Beef and Oatmeal Breakfast

- 2 cups cooked, ground beef (lean)
- 1 cup cooked oatmeal
- 1/2 cup steamed blueberries
- 1/2 cup plain yogurt
- 1 tablespoon olive oil

14. Pork and Apple Stew

- 2 cups cooked, ground pork (lean)
- 1 cup cooked brown rice
- 1/2 cup steamed apples, diced
- 1/2 cup steamed carrots, diced
- 1 tablespoon flaxseed oil

15. Lamb and Couscous Salad

- 2 cups cooked, ground lamb
- 1 cup cooked couscous
- 1/2 cup steamed peas
- 1/2 cup steamed carrots, diced
- 1 tablespoon coconut oil

16. Venison and Vegetable Stir-Fry

- 2 cups cooked, ground venison
- 1 cup cooked brown rice

- 1/2 cup steamed broccoli, chopped
- 1/2 cup steamed carrots, sliced
- 1 tablespoon fish oil

17. Duck and Sweet Potato Casserole

- 2 cups cooked, shredded duck
- 1 cup cooked, mashed sweet potato
- 1/2 cup steamed peas
- 1/2 cup steamed carrots, diced
- 1 tablespoon olive oil

18. Bison and Veggie Patties

- 2 cups cooked, ground bison
- 1 cup cooked quinoa
- 1/2 cup steamed zucchini, grated
- 1/2 cup steamed carrots, grated
- 1 tablespoon flaxseed oil
- Form into small patties and serve

Preparation Tips:

- Always remove bones and excess fat from meats.
- Cook all ingredients thoroughly to ensure safety and digestibility.
- Cool the meals before serving to your dog.
- Store leftovers in the refrigerator for up to 3 days or freeze for longer storage.

Note: These recipes are designed for dogs with normal digestion. Always consult with a veterinarian before making significant changes to your dog's diet, especially if they have specific health conditions or dietary requirements.

Homemade Dog Food Recipes for

Dogs with Digestive Disorders

1. Gentle Chicken and Rice

- 2 cups boiled, shredded chicken breast (skinless)
- 1 cup cooked white rice
- 1 tablespoon pumpkin puree (unsweetened)
- 1/4 teaspoon ground ginger

2. Soothing Turkey and Oatmeal

- 2 cups boiled, ground turkey (lean)
- 1 cup cooked oatmeal
- 1/2 cup steamed carrots, mashed
- 1 tablespoon plain yogurt

3. Low-Fat Beef and Potato Stew

- 2 cups boiled, lean ground beef
- 1 cup cooked, cubed potatoes (skinless)
- 1/2 cup steamed green beans, chopped
- 1 tablespoon flaxseed oil

4. Digestible Fish and Sweet Potato

- 2 cups boiled, flaked whitefish (e.g., cod)
- 1 cup cooked, mashed sweet potato
- 1/2 cup steamed zucchini, diced
- 1 tablespoon coconut oil

5. Hypoallergenic Rabbit and Pumpkin

- 2 cups boiled, ground rabbit
- 1 cup pureed pumpkin (unsweetened)
- 1/2 cup cooked quinoa
- 1 tablespoon olive oil

6. Lamb and Rice Porridge

- 2 cups boiled, ground lamb (lean)
- 1 cup cooked white rice
- 1/2 cup steamed carrots, mashed
- 1 tablespoon fish oil

7. Venison and Pea Soup

- 2 cups boiled, ground venison
- 1 cup cooked green peas (mashed for easier digestion)
- 1 cup low-sodium beef or venison broth
- 1 tablespoon sunflower oil

8. Duck and Potato Puree

- 2 cups boiled, shredded duck (lean)
- 1 cup cooked, mashed potatoes (skinless)
- 1/2 cup steamed green beans, diced
- 1 tablespoon hemp oil

9. Bison and Barley Broth

- 2 cups boiled, ground bison
- 1 cup cooked barley
- 1/2 cup steamed pumpkin, mashed

- 1 tablespoon flaxseed oil

10. Turkey and Rice Meatballs

- 2 cups boiled, ground turkey (lean)
- 1 cup cooked white rice
- 1/2 cup steamed carrots, diced
- 1 tablespoon coconut oil
- Form into small meatballs and serve

11. Chicken Liver and Oatmeal Mash

- 1 cup boiled, chopped chicken liver
- 1 cup cooked oatmeal
- 1/2 cup steamed zucchini, mashed
- 1 tablespoon olive oil

12. Salmon and Sweet Potato Cakes

- 2 cups boiled, flaked salmon
- 1 cup cooked, mashed sweet potato
- 1/2 cup cooked quinoa
- 1 tablespoon fish oil
- Form into small patties and serve

13. Pork and Apple Stew

- 2 cups boiled, ground pork (lean)
- 1 cup cooked brown rice
- 1/2 cup steamed apples, diced
- 1 tablespoon sunflower oil

14. Beef and Carrot Soup

- 2 cups boiled, lean ground beef
- 1 cup low-sodium beef broth
- 1/2 cup steamed carrots, mashed
- 1 tablespoon flaxseed oil

15. Whitefish and Rice Pudding

- 2 cups boiled, flaked whitefish (e.g., tilapia)
- 1 cup cooked white rice
- 1/2 cup plain yogurt
- 1 tablespoon coconut oil

16. Lamb and Spinach Puree

- 2 cups boiled, ground lamb (lean)
- 1 cup cooked, mashed spinach
- 1 cup cooked white rice
- 1 tablespoon olive oil

17. Chicken and Sweet Potato Soup

- 2 cups boiled, shredded chicken breast (skinless)
- 1 cup cooked, mashed sweet potato
- 1 cup low-sodium chicken broth
- 1 tablespoon fish oil

18. Turkey and Pumpkin Patties

- 2 cups boiled, ground turkey (lean)
- 1 cup pureed pumpkin (unsweetened)
- 1/2 cup cooked quinoa
- 1 tablespoon sunflower oil
- Form into small patties and serve

Preparation Tips:

- Always remove bones and excess fat from meats.
- Cook all ingredients thoroughly to ensure safety and digestibility.
- Cool the meals before serving to your dog.
- Store leftovers in the refrigerator for up to 3 days or freeze for longer storage.

Note: These recipes are designed for dogs with known digestive disorders, illnesses, or issues. Always consult with a veterinarian before making significant changes to your dog's diet, especially if they have specific health conditions or dietary requirements.

****

Chapter 13

Dietary Supplements For Cats and Dogs

Dietary Supplements for Cats and Dogs:

Administration and Sourcing

Dietary supplements can play a crucial role in maintaining and enhancing the health of cats and dogs, especially those with digestive issues. They can provide essential nutrients that may be missing from their diet, support specific health needs, and promote overall well-being.

1. Types of Dietary Supplements for Cats and Dogs

- **Multivitamins**: Provide a balanced range of vitamins and minerals to support general health.
- **Probiotics**: Beneficial bacteria that support gut health and aid in digestion.
- **Omega-3 Fatty Acids**: Found in fish oil supplements, they support skin, coat, and joint health.
- **Antioxidants**: Such as vitamins E and C, which help combat oxidative stress and support the immune system.
- **Joint Supplements**: Containing glucosamine, chondroitin, and MSM to support joint health and mobility.
- **Digestive Enzymes**: Aid in the breakdown and absorption of nutrients.
- **Fiber Supplements**: Help regulate bowel movements and support digestive health.

- **Amino Acids**: Like taurine for cats, which is essential for heart and eye health.

2. Administering Supplements to Your Pets

- **Consultation with a Veterinarian**: Always consult with a veterinarian before starting any supplement regimen to ensure it's appropriate for your pet's specific needs and health status.
- **Dosage and Frequency**: Follow the recommended dosage and frequency on the supplement label or as advised by your veterinarian.
- **Mixing with Food**: Many supplements can be mixed with your pet's food for easy administration. Ensure the food is palatable to encourage consumption.
- **Using Treats**: Some supplements come in treat form or can be disguised in a favorite treat to make administration easier.
- **Liquid and Pill Forms**: Liquid supplements can be added to food or water, while pills may need to be hidden in food or a pill pocket.
- **Monitoring**: Observe your pet for any adverse reactions or side effects and adjust the supplement regimen as necessary.

3. Sourcing Quality Supplements for Cats and Dogs

- **Veterinary Recommendations**: Your veterinarian can recommend reputable brands and specific supplements that are suited to your pet's needs.
- **Pet Specialty Stores**: These stores often carry a wide range of supplements specifically designed for pets.
- **Online Retailers**: Websites specializing in pet health products can offer a variety of supplements with detailed

product information and reviews.

- **Pharmacies**: Some pharmacies carry pet supplements, especially those that are also suitable for human consumption, like fish oil.
- **Manufacturers' Websites**: Purchasing directly from the manufacturer's website can ensure authenticity and provide access to detailed product information.

4. Considerations for Supplement Use in Pets

- **Quality and Purity**: Look for supplements that have been third-party tested for purity and potency.
- **Ingredient Sources**: Opt for supplements with high-quality, natural ingredients and avoid unnecessary fillers or artificial additives.
- **Formulation for Pets**: Choose supplements specifically formulated for cats or dogs, as their nutritional needs differ from humans.
- **Interaction with Medications**: Be aware of potential interactions between supplements and any medications your pet is taking.

5. Special Considerations for Cats and Dogs with Digestive Issues

- **Probiotics and Prebiotics**: These can be particularly beneficial for pets with digestive disorders, helping to restore and maintain a healthy gut microbiome.
- **Digestive Enzymes**: May aid pets with enzyme deficiencies or those with difficulty digesting certain nutrients.
- **Fiber Supplements**: Can help manage conditions like diarrhea or constipation by regulating bowel movements.

Dietary supplements can be a valuable addition to your cat or dog's diet, particularly for those with digestive issues. However, it's essential to choose the right supplements, administer them correctly, and source them from reputable suppliers. Always consult with your veterinarian to ensure that any supplements you provide are safe and appropriate for your pet's specific health needs. By doing so, you can support your pet's health and well-being through targeted nutritional supplementation.

****

Chapter 14

Homemade Cat and Dog Food:

Meal Planning and Preparation Tips

Creating homemade meals for cats and dogs with digestive issues requires careful planning and preparation. By following specific guidelines, pet owners can ensure that their furry friends receive nutritious, balanced, and easily digestible meals.

1. Understanding Nutritional Needs

- **Species-Specific Requirements**: Cats are obligate carnivores, while dogs are omnivores. Their nutritional needs differ significantly, and meals should be formulated accordingly.
- **Balanced Diet**: A balanced diet includes appropriate proportions of proteins, fats, carbohydrates, vitamins, minerals, and water.
- **Special Considerations**: For pets with digestive issues, focus on easily digestible ingredients and avoid known irritants or allergens.

2. Ingredient Selection

- **High-Quality Proteins**: Choose lean meats like chicken, turkey, beef, and fish. For cats, include organ meats for essential nutrients like taurine.
- **Digestible Carbohydrates**: Opt for cooked, easily digestible carbohydrates like rice, sweet potatoes, and oats.

- **Vegetables and Fruits**: Incorporate steamed or pureed vegetables and fruits for fiber and nutrients. Avoid onions, garlic, grapes, and raisins, which can be toxic to pets.
- **Healthy Fats**: Include sources of omega-3 and omega-6 fatty acids, such as fish oil, flaxseed oil, or coconut oil, for skin and coat health.

3. Meal Planning

- **Rotating Ingredients**: Rotate protein sources and vegetables to provide a variety of nutrients and prevent boredom.
- **Portion Sizes**: Determine appropriate portion sizes based on your pet's weight, age, activity level, and health condition.
- **Supplements**: Consult with a veterinarian or pet nutritionist to identify any necessary supplements to ensure nutritional completeness.

4. Preparation Techniques

- **Cooking Methods**: Boil, steam, or bake ingredients to ensure they are easily digestible. Avoid frying or using heavy oils.
- **Food Safety**: Practice safe food handling by washing hands and utensils, avoiding cross-contamination, and cooking meats to proper temperatures.
- **Consistency**: Blend or puree ingredients for cats and dogs with severe digestive issues to aid in digestion.

5. Storage and Serving

- **Cooling and Storing**: Allow cooked meals to cool before serving. Store leftovers in airtight containers in the refrigerator for up to 3 days or freeze for longer-term storage.

- **Thawing and Reheating**: Thaw frozen meals in the refrigerator and reheat gently to avoid nutrient loss. Ensure the food is at a safe temperature before serving.

6. Transitioning to Homemade Diets

- **Gradual Transition**: Slowly introduce homemade meals by mixing them with your pet's current food and gradually increasing the proportion over a week.
- **Monitoring**: Observe your pet's reaction to the new diet, including their stool quality, energy levels, and overall health.

7. Sample Meal Plans

- **Day 1**: Chicken and rice with steamed carrots and a spoonful of pumpkin puree.
- **Day 2**: Turkey and sweet potato with steamed green beans and a drizzle of flaxseed oil.
- **Day 3**: Beef and oatmeal with steamed zucchini and a sprinkle of ground eggshell for calcium.

8. Addressing Digestive Issues

- **Bland Diets**: For acute digestive upset, temporarily feed a bland diet of boiled chicken and rice until symptoms improve.
- **Fiber Adjustment**: Adjust fiber levels based on your pet's needs, using pumpkin or sweet potato for constipation and rice or oats for diarrhea.

9. Variety and Treats

- **Variety**: Introduce new ingredients gradually to ensure they are well-tolerated and to add variety to your pet's diet.

- **Homemade Treats**: Create healthy treats using ingredients from your pet's meals, such as dehydrated meat or baked vegetable crisps.

10. Ongoing Evaluation

- **Regular Check-ups**: Schedule regular check-ups with your veterinarian to monitor your pet's health and nutritional status.
- **Adjustments**: Be prepared to make adjustments to the diet based on your pet's evolving needs and any changes in their health condition.

Meal planning and preparation for homemade cat and dog food require a thoughtful approach, especially for pets with digestive issues. By understanding nutritional needs, selecting appropriate ingredients, and following safe preparation and storage practices, pet owners can provide their companions with nutritious and enjoyable meals.

****

Other Books By This Author

Unleash Your Calm:

Navigating Life's Storms With Grace and Inner Peace

Ancient Healthy Recipes for Modern Plates:

The Real Mediterranean Diet Unveiled

Know When To Pivot:

Navigating Uncertainty With Confidence

Rise Above:

Breaking Chains to Overcome Unhealthy Habits

Embracing a More Fulfilling Life

Gluten Free Mexican Recipes:

Enjoying The Flavours of Ol' Mexico

Rising from the Ashes:

Reclaiming Your Life after Narcissistic Abuse

Beyond The Agony Of Chronic Pain:

Finding Relief and Understanding

Release Your Greatness:

Breaking Free To Live A Purposeful...Limitless Life

Rest Now My Love:

Coping With The Loss Of A Life Partner

Failing Forward – Rising Stronger!

Rekindling Hope In A Crazy World

Daring To Dream A Bigger...Better Dream

Why He Doesn't Love You Anymore

Reshaping Your World – When Relationships Require Necessary Endings

The Emotions Mastery Handbook:

Mastering Your Emotional Intelligence for a Life of Fulfillment

Wild Savory Adventures:

Mastering the Art of Cooking Wild Game

AI Prompt Power:

Unleashing AI To Create Passive Income

From Lot To Loot:

A Comprehensive Guide to "No-Money-Down" Land Flipping Deals in America

Excelling In The Face of Personal Chaos

A Very Plain Amish Christmas Cookbook

****

About the Author

James C. Tanner is a highly published writer, who has written and published for over 38 years.

He has written and taught under contract, business skills development programs for clients such as, The Government of Canada.

He is a former professional Investigator who specialized in cult/occult related matters, with a targeted focus on the ritual slaughter of animals.

With a writing portfolio which includes many genres, James C. Tanner has written heavily in areas of business, relationships, psychology, personal motivation and human interest.

Over the course of years, James C. Tanner has published almost exclusively under pen names utilizing 5 different pen names, each assigned to specific writing genres. In recent years, he has begun to publish under his own name.

Today, James C. Tanner lives the quiet life of a writer tucked away in the vineyard country of Kelowna, British Columbia, Canada.

Read more at https://www.jamesctanner.com.

www.ingramcontent.com/pod-product-compliance
Lightning Source LLC
Chambersburg PA
CBHW021213160726
47994CB00001B/466